Fruit Key and Twig Key to Trees and Shrubs

Fruit Key to Northeastern Trees

Twig Key to the Deciduous Woody Plants of Eastern North America

William M. Harlow, Ph. D.

Professor of Wood Technology
State University of New York
College of Forestry
Syracuse, New York

Dover Publications, Inc.
New York

Published in Canada by General Publishing Company, Ltd., 30 Lesmill Road, Don Mills, Toronto, Ontario.
Published in the United Kingdom by Constable and Company, Ltd., 10 Orange Street, London WC 2.

This Dover edition, first published in 1959, is an unabridged and unaltered republication of the first (1946) edition of *Fruit Key to Northeastern Trees*, and the fourth revised (1954) edition of *Twig Key to the Deciduous Woody Plants of Eastern North America*. Both books were originally published by the author.

Standard Book Number: 486-20511-8
Library of Congress Catalog Card Number: 59-9671

Manufactured in the United States of America
Dover Publications, Inc.
180 Varick Street
New York, N.Y. 10014

FRONTISPIECE

Northern White Pine Cones ×3/4
(Small first season's cones above, large
two year mature cones below)

Fruit Key to Northeastern Trees

By
WILLIAM M. HARLOW, PH.D.
Professor of Wood Technology
State University of New York
College of Forestry
Syracuse, New York

Dover Publications, Inc.

PREFACE

For a number of years, my students and others have used "Twig Key to the Deciduous Woody Plants of Eastern North America" in their studies of winter twigs. The suggestion has been made that a similar key to fruits might be useful. The following introduction and key are presented, therefore, in the hope that they may help to awaken an interest in the many diverse fruit forms produced by our northeastern trees.

Someone has said that a seed is a young plant carefully wrapped up, and waiting to go somewhere. The manner in which fruits and seeds are disseminated comprises a fascinating chapter of natural history. Thoreau once remarked that most fruits or seeds have wings of some sort or other, — even those of the cherry.

The key is intended to serve not only in the actual identification of fruits, but also as an instructional medium. For this reason most technical terms used are explained parenthetically.

In several genera, such as *Salix*, *Malus*, and *Crataegus*, no attempt is made to separate the various species since this is a field for the specialist.

With few exceptions, the illustrations are taken from "Textbook of Dendrology" by W.M. Harlow and E.S. Harrar. For this courtesy, grateful acknowledgment is made to the publishers, the McGraw-Hill Book Co., and the co-author, Dr. E.S. Harrar.

Syracuse, N.Y.
August, 1946   William M. Harlow

INTRODUCTION

Before attempting to describe some of the more common fruits, it is necessary to ask the question "what is a fruit?" It might seem to be a simple matter to agree upon a definition, but careful comparison of various books on plants indicates that even the experts do not always interpret certain structures in the same way, or at least are not consistent in what they name them. The author of one book, for instance, calls the fruit of the birch a cone, while another author refers to it as a minute winged nutlet borne in a cone-like structure.

Perhaps the easiest definition is that a fruit is the seed-bearing portion of the plant. This is a little better than the small boy's suggestion that "Fruits is what you eats", but still leaves much to be desired as a precise technical definition. Another complicating factor is size. When a fruit is extremely small, like that of the birch, and is borne in great numbers in a cone-like structure, which itself is less than an inch long, even trained botanists are inclined to call the cone a fruit. The average untrained observer certainly would refer to the tiny winged nutlets (fruits) as "seeds". Finally, the word "fruit" is used by everyone, and each individual thinks he knows its meaning anyway. Our problem is to take a popular word and try to give it a precise technical meaning.

CONIFEROUS FRUITS.

The narrow-leaved evergreens, or conifers, belong to a group of trees, ancient in lineage, known as the Gymnosperms. This name was happily chosen since it means "naked seed", and is thus descriptive of what we find when we examine the fruit. All of the conifers, included in the key, produce cones, even though in one or two cases, the appearance is more like that of a "berry". When the cone scales open, the seeds are revealed lying "naked" upon them, and not surrounded by any sort of containing structure.

The life history of cones, especially those of the pines,

has some interesting chapters. Like most if not all of the conifers, the brilliant red female flowers[1] are borne erect on the
branch. By the end of the first growing season they become
small inconspicuous green cones. Either that autumn or the
following spring, these slowly turn over, assume a pendent position, and during this second season grow to maturity. They
may then either open and release their seeds, or remain closed
for months or years, depending upon the species. Pitch pine
cones open gradually during the winter, and drop their seeds upon the snow where many are eaten by birds who would otherwise
find it more difficult to obtain food. The cones of the jack pine
often remain closed for many years, and require heat such as
that from a moderate ground fire, to open them. When this happens,
the stored seeds of perhaps twenty years are released nearly at
the same time and this may result in dense even-aged stands of
young trees. In the absence of sufficient heat, some of the closed
cones become entombed in the trunk as the growing tissues cover
them over completely. Later, when the trunk is sawed, these embedded cones are exposed, and some of their seeds will germinate when planted.

   Not all of the "conifers" have cones. The yew (shrubby in
the region covered by the key) has a bright scarlet fleshy seed.
The flesh is edible, with a pleasant but somewhat sickish-sweet
taste. The seed itself, however, should not be cracked between
the teeth since the "meat" within, like the leaves and other
parts of the plant, contains a bitter poisonous alkaloid.

ANGIOSPERMOUS FRUITS.

   The broadleaved trees belong to another group of plants
known as the Angiosperms in which the seeds are borne enclosed
in an ovary. The Angiosperms are divided into the Monocoty-
ledons, such as the grasses, corn, and palms; and the Dicoty-
ledons including thousands of herbs, vines, shrubs, and trees.
Compared to the more primitive conifers, the Angiosperms present an amazing array of diverse fruit forms, and it is in this
group that a proper definition of the word "fruit" becomes more
difficult.

   [1]Many botanists do not call the reproductive organs in the conifers, flowers.
The term is used here for convenience.

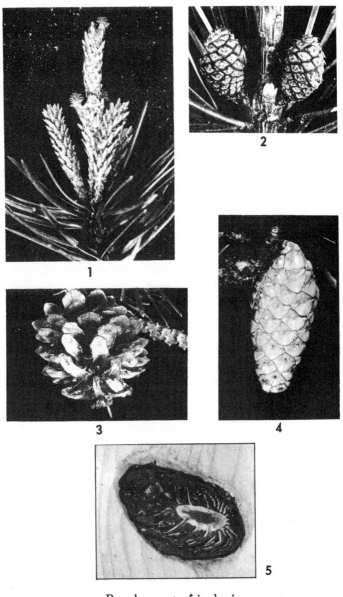

Development of jack pine cones.
1. Three female flowers catching wind-borne pollen.
2. Two of the same at the end of the first season.
3. An old cone from which the seeds have been shed.
4. Mature cone at the end of the second season.
5. Cone embedded in the trunk wood.

(This page courtesy "American Forests".)

The characteristic female flower structure of the broadleaved tree is the pistil. Sometimes the pistil is easily seen and
recognized with the naked eye. It may, however, be extremely
small so that a hand lens is necessary. Further, many pistils
may occur in a compact cluster so that one is not readily dis-
tinguished from another. To name properly the type of fruit, it is
often necessary to trace its development from the pistil.

The lower part of the pistil is called the ovary. It contains a cavity, and attached to the walls of the cavity are the
ovules which upon fertilization become the *seeds*. The cavity
may be single, or it may be divided into several smaller chambers
by partitions. When so divided, the ovary or pistil is called *compound*. The *simple* type has no partitions, but in certain species
a single cavity may not signify a simple pistil. A definition of
the word fruit may now be proposed. *A fruit is a ripened ovary*
together with any appendages or dried flower parts which it still
may retain. Notice that the *flower* develops into the *fruit*, the
fertilized *ovule* becomes the *seed*. This is important to remember,
and when you look at something or other of a fruiting nature you
must always ask yourself the question "Is this a fruit or is it a
seed, and how do I know which it is?" Unless you are this critical you will soon be lost in the maze of multitudinous fruit and
seed forms of even our common trees.

COMPOUND FRUITS.

When several to many pistils are compacted, the result is a
compound fruit. These are of two sorts. In such trees as magnolia, and yellowpoplar (Pages 27 & 35) many pistils are borne
in a cone-like structure within a *single* large flower. The result-
ing fruit is said to be *aggregate*. The other condition is where a
number of small *separate* flowers *each* with its pistil (s) are
borne close together. Here the result is a *multiple* which characterizes such trees as the sycamore and sweetgum (Page 35).

A female flower of a willow ×30. Actually only about a quarter of an inch long, many of these are borne together forming a catkin. The conspicuous part of this flower is the pistil.

SIMPLE FRUITS.

Fruits which develop from a single pistil may be classified
in one of several ways. They may be *dry*, or *fleshy*, but in certain
cases this is not easy to ascertain, since the flesh not only may
be thin, but also so hard and firm that it is not recognized as
flesh. If fleshy, the fruit is probably a *drupe*, *berry*, or *pome*. It
is easier to give well known examples of these than it is to give
definite features by which an unknown fruit may be classified.
Again this is because it is necessary to trace the development
of the fruit from its precursor, the flower.

Drupe — Botanically, this is a fleshy fruit in which the
inner ovary wall is hard and bony, the outer one soft and fleshy.
Common examples are the prune, cherry, peach, plum, and almond.
A drupe usually has one pit, but may have two. Some fruits such
as those of the walnuts and basswoods are said to be "drupaceous". This means that man confronted with a tremendous
number of natural forms, tries to pigeonhole them for easy ref-
erence, but every once in a while he comes across some form
which is neither one thing nor the other. In the cases mentioned,
the "flesh" is almost dry, or nearly hard and woody, hence the
term drupaceous which is merely a device for getting out of an
awkward situation.

Berry — The definition is easy, but the term is greatly cor-
rupted due to popular usage. A berry is a fleshy fruit in which
both inner and outer ovary walls are fleshy, and the seeds are
distributed throughout. Some common examples are blueberry,
and huckleberry (these are not synonymous), gooseberry, tomato,
and persimmon. Strawberry, blackberry, raspberry and mulberry
are not "berries", according to the above definition, but are compound fruits made up of many small units (mostly druplets).
Careful inspection will show that this is so. Although a berry is
usually several-seeded, it may contain only one seed. If this
seed has a hard heavy seed coat, the fruit may be mistaken for a
drupe.

Pome — Here, the outer ovary wall is fleshy, the inner one papery, or like cartilage. Everyone, in eating apple pie, has rasped his tongue with these sharp cartilaginous portions of the inner ovary wall incompletely removed by the cook, or apple processer. Incidentally the pome is derived from a compound pistil, and the enlarged receptacle is also a part of it (slice an apple in half lengthwise and see for yourself). The drupe and berry are from simple pistils. Some common pomes in addition to the apple are those of pear, shadbush, mountainash, and hawthorn (thornapple).

Dry fruits are conveniently classified by observing whether at maturity they split along definite seams (sutures). If they split, they are called dehiscent, if they do not, they are said to be indehiscent. The three common dry dehiscent fruits are the *legume*, *follicle*, and *capsule*.

Legume — This is the product of a simple pistil, and cracks open along two sutures. Examples include the bean, pea, clover, blacklocust and coffeetree.

Follicle — This fruit, also from a simple pistil breaks along only one suture. Single follicles are not found on the trees covered by this key, but in magnolia the fruit is an aggregate of follicles. (Page 35)

Capsule — The capsule, in contrast to the legume and follicle, comes from a compound pistil, and may open in one of several ways. Common examples are the poppy, lilac, catalpa, and horsechestnut, even though most people think of the latter as a "nut".

The dry indehiscent fruits found on trees covered by the key, are the *achene*, *samara*, and *nut*.

Achene — This is a small, unwinged, but sometimes plumed, one-celled, one-seeded fruit. In sycamore, many achenes are compounded to form the globose head characteristic of this tree. (Page 35)

Samara — The samara is similar to the achene except that it has a thin membranous wing extending terminally, or surrounding the seed cavity. Common examples are those of the maple, ash, and elm.

Nut — Botanically, the nut is not difficult to define, but it is not always easy to recognize, or to separate from certain other types. A typical nut is partially or wholly enclosed in a husk which may be papery, leafy, woody, or spiny in character. The nut itself has a bony, or leathery outer wall and is usually one-seeded by abortion. This means that more than one ovule may be present but commonly only one develops. Examples include the chestnut, oak (acorn), beech, hickory, and hornbeam. Superficially, the fruit of the horsechestnut would seem to fit the description, but actually there is no husk, and that which appears to be a husk is the outer ovary wall of a capsule. This is a very good example of the fact that things are not always what they seem to be, and highlights the importance of not making snap decisions before getting all available evidence.

FRUITING HABITS

Although autumn would seem an appropriate time to look for fruits and seeds, certain species fruit in the late spring. Included in this group are the three northeastern elms, the soft maples (red and silver), red birch, and the willows and poplars. Most of these trees are commonly found along water courses where the spring-maturing seeds find fresh, moist, alluvial soil waiting to receive them. Seeds of the willows and poplars germinate within two or three days, an interesting fact which can be verified by placing a few of them upon a moist blotter covered with a water glass.

Trees usually do not produce seed until they have reached a considerable size, but in a few species such as jack pine, cones may be produced when the tree is only two to three feet high.

There may be more than one answer to the question "why doesn't my tree bear fruit?" These are some of the possibilities:

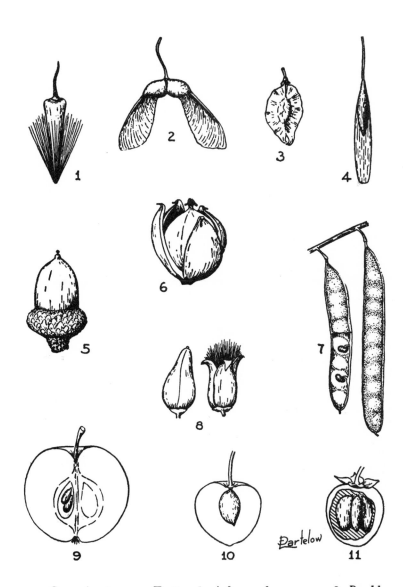

Some Angiosperm Fruits. *1. Achene* of sycamore. *2. Double samara* of maple. *3. Single samara* of elm. *4. Single samara* of ash. *5. Acorn (nut)* of oak. *6. Nut* of hickory. *7. Legume* of black locust. *8. Capsule* of poplar. *9. Pome* of apple. *10. Drupe* of cherry. *11. Berry* of persimmon.

(1) the tree still is too young; (2) male flowers are borne on trees separate from those bearing female ones and the tree in question may be a male; (3) a late frost destroyed the flowers; (4) it may be an "off" year. Some species produce flowers and fruit every year, but others are characterized by extremely heavy crops followed by several seasons when not a single flower can be found on an entire tree. Sugar maple is one of these, and over large areas almost every tree will appear covered with a bright yellow "mist" caused by countless thousands of flowers. Two or more years will then pass before the next appearance of any flowers or fruit at all. Usually an occasional tree is "out of step" with the rest, and such an individual flowers and fruits during the "off" years.

HOW TREES TRAVEL.

You may say that trees do not travel, since one of the most obvious differences between the higher plants and animals is that the plants remain rooted while the animals are free to move from one place to another. Although an individual tree, in the absence of accidents (including man), may grow to maturity on the spot where the fruit or seed was deposited, one or both of these structures often have developed special ways of travelling long distances. By means of their offspring, then, trees are able to move about and change their location from one generation to the next.

For many millions of years the fruits and/or seeds of certain species have been airborne, often for considerable distances. Some, like those of the ashes and maples, have thin, membranous wings, and although these fruits are relatively heavy, they may, if released at a sufficient height, ride a strong wind a hundred yards or more.

The flask-shaped fruits of the willows and poplars release tiny seeds which are about the size of a pinhead. These are equipped with a parachute of silky or cottony floss, and will float for many miles, even in a light breeze. Some of the tropical jungle trees have remarkable airborne seeds. One of the writer's

SUMMARY OF FRUIT TYPES

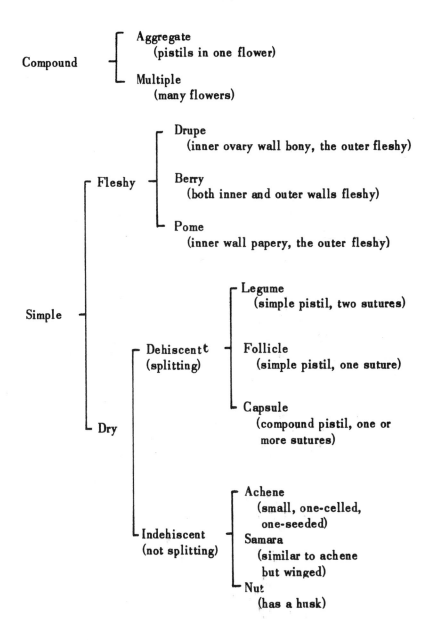

Compound
- Aggregate (pistils in one flower)
- Multiple (many flowers)

Simple
- Fleshy
  - Drupe (inner ovary wall bony, the outer fleshy)
  - Berry (both inner and outer walls fleshy)
  - Pome (inner wall papery, the outer fleshy)
- Dry
  - Dehiscent (splitting)
    - Legume (simple pistil, two sutures)
    - Follicle (simple pistil, one suture)
    - Capsule (compound pistil, one or more sutures)
  - Indehiscent (not splitting)
    - Achene (small, one-celled, one-seeded)
    - Samara (similar to achene but winged)
    - Nut (has a husk)

students found himself surrounded by graceful, silvery-winged
"gliders" with a five inch wing span, sailing and dipping downward from the tops of tall trees in the New Guinea forest.

Some trees rely upon another sort of wing for the dispersal
of their fruits or seeds. It is no accident that common hedgerow
species include the various cherries, dogwoods, poison-ivy, buckthorn and wild grape. Sometimes certain shrubs are found in seemingly strange places. When scouting for gooseberry or currant
bushes (white pine blister rust control), it is customary to scruti-
nize the lower forks of old trees since *Ribes* bushes are commonly found there. The writer knows of one gooseberry bush which
has flourished for at least twenty-five years in the fork of an old
sugar maple. Nearby are similar "sites" bearing red elder bushes
ten feet above the ground. The only reasonable explanation seems
to be that the seeds were left there by birds.

Sometimes flocks of starlings roost by the thousands in
young pine plantations. Just at dusk these birds blacken the sky
and disappear into the tops of the trees until it is hard to see
how any more could be sheltered. After dark if one approaches
the roosting birds, and raps one of the trees with a stick, there
is a roar of wings which must be heard to be appreciated. The
area smells like a chicken roost, and considerable nitrogenous
material is deposited, so much so that whole sections of the
plantation may be killed. A year or more later, thousands of
seedlings spring up, principally those of buckthorn, but the
cherries, mulberry, and other fleshy fruited species are also
found. Within a few years there results a thicket of "weed"
trees through which it is difficult to walk. The fact that birds
eat certain fruits has thus resulted in a complete change from
a pure coniferous stand to one of hardwoods (broadleaved), and
worthless ones at that.

Fruit or seeds without wings are distributed in other ways.
A great many acorns and other nuts are planted by squirrels even
though they exact a considerable levy in so doing. Acorns of the
white oaks germinate in the autumn and almost depend upon the
squirrels to plant them before they are frozen. Large fruits like

those of the walnuts and hickories may roll downhill, and in this way "travel". Under proper conditions, many fruits may float or be carried by running water and eventually germinate many miles away from the parent tree. Finally, perhaps the greatest seed dispersing agent is man himself who crosses oceans and continents, and mixes introduced species with the native until an observer lacking adequate records might not be able to tell one from the other.

POISON-SUMAC *Toxicodendron vernix (L.) Kuntze*

Although the *ripe* whitish fruit is said to be devoid of the poisonous resin found in special canals scattered throughout the rest of the plant, it is thought best not to include the fruit in the key. Careful scrutiny of the illustration on Page 14 will enable anyone to recognize these fruits. They are borne on a large swamp shrub or small tree, with alternate compound leaves which turn to a brilliant scarlet in autumn. If any part of the plant is bruised and the canals broken so that the sticky resin touches the skin, dermatitis will probably result. *

Twig and fruit of poison-sumac

–NOTES–

Triad of White Oak Acorns
(Enlarged)

HOW TO USE THE KEY

When the user must choose one of two alternatives, a key is said to be *dichotomous*, and this is the type used here. Let us suppose that you have picked up the fruit illustrated below, and wish to discover its identity. Turn to the next page and read the two alternatives offered at No. 1. If you have studied the "Introduction" you will see at once that the fruit is not a cone, and you are directed to turn to No. 27. The fruit is not winged, hence you follow the second part of No. 27 to No. 44. At No. 44, it is evident that your unknown fruit is not fleshy, and this brings you to No. 76. The fruit is not compound and so you next consult No. 80. At No. 80 it is evident that the fruit is not an acorn, and the second part of No. 80 brings you to No. 97. Here it is clear that the fruit is not a pod, and it is hoped you will recognize it as a leathery nut enclosed by a husk. If so, you should proceed to No. 98. The fruit is more than one half inch in diameter which takes you to No. 101. Since the husk splits, 102 is consulted. The nut is encased in a prickly husk, so you turn to No. 103. This must be the end of the trail since there is no way of going further. The nut is triangular in cross-section, and after comparing the unknown with the illustrations, there should be no doubt concerning its identity.

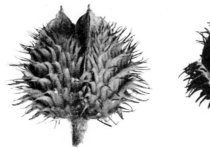

×2

KEY TO TREE FRUITS

(Illustrations are at ¾ natural size unless otherwise stated)

1. Fruit a cone or cone-like, featured by overlapping scales - - - - - 2
1. Fruit not a cone - 27

    2. Cone scales opposite (paired); cones small, mostly less
       than ½" long - 3
    2. Cone scales alternate (in spirals); cones mostly more
       than ½" long - 5
3. Cones oblong, at maturity yellowish brown — Arborvitae or
Northern White-cedar *Thuja occidentalis* L.
3. Cones globose, at maturity bluish or purplish - - - - - - - - - - - - - 4

    4. Cone fleshy (usually not recognized as a cone); seeds wing-
       less - - Eastern Redcedar or Redcedar Juniper *Juniperus
       virginiana* L. 2
    4. Cones semi-fleshy, each scale with a small "spike" in the
       center, seeds winged - - Southern or Atlantic white-cedar
       Chamaecyparis thyoides (L.) B. S. P. 3, 4

5. Fruits or seeds have a terminal (end) wing* - - - - - - - - - - - - - - 6
5. Fruits or seeds have two lateral (side) wings
or may seem unwinged - 22

    6. Cone falls to pieces at maturity leaving the spike-like cone
       axis upright on the branch - 7
    6. Cone scales persistent - 8

7. Cone consisting of terminally winged units, 4-angled at the
base - - Tuliptree or Yellow-poplar *Liriodendron tulipifera* L.
(See No. 37)
7. Cone consisting of flat scales, each bearing two winged seeds -
Balsam Fir *Abies balsamea* (L.) Mill. 7

    8. Small pointed bracts visible between scales near base of
       cone; cone upright on tree (Larches) - - - - - - - - - - - - - - - - 9
    8. Bracts not visible or lacking; cone pendent on tree - - - - - - - 10

*If something resembling a cone has nutlets or seeds which are them-
selves *wingless*, probably the tree is a hornbeam (See No. 100); or a magnolia
(See No. 78).

9. Cones about 5/8'' long -- Tamarack *Larix laricina* (DuRoi) K. Koch. **5**

9. Cones from 1'' to 1¼'' long -- European Larch *Larix decidua* Mill. **6**

10. Cone scales more or less thickened (Pines) - - - - - - - - - - 11

10. Cone scales almost paper-thin (Spruces and Hemlocks) - - - 18

11. Cones 4'' to 8'' long, long-stalked; -- White Pine *Pinus strobus* L. **12**

11. Cones less than 4'' long, short-stalked, or stalk lacking (sessile) - 12

12. Cones unsymmetrical (lop-sided), usually remaining closed at maturity -- Jack Pine *Pinus banksiana* Lamb. **11**

12. Cones symmetrical, opening at maturity or during the following season - 13

13. Cone scales unarmed (no prickles), or prickles indistinct - - - - - 14

13. Cone scales with definite prickles - - - - - - - - - - - - - - - - - 15

(Nos. 1 to 4 are shown at 3 times natural size)

x 1/2

14. Scales unarmed, the outer surfaces more or less smooth
and rounded -- Red or Norway Pine *Pinus resinosa* Ait. **13**
14. Scales with raised pyramid-shaped tips sometimes
bearing small indistinct prickles - - Scotch Pine
Pinus sylvestris L. **14**

15. Prickles claw-like, stout -- Table-Mountain Pine *Pinus pungens*
Lamb. **15**
15. Prickles small and more slender - 16

16. Prickles very slender, sometimes falling off; closed
cones more or less oblong -- Shortleaf Pine *Pinus*
echinata Mill. **8**
16. Prickles conspicuous; cones more egg-shaped (ovoid) - - - - 17

17. Open cones tend to be flat at the base; needles in 3s -- Pitch Pine
Pinus rigida Mill. **9**
17. Open cones more or less rounded at the base; needles in 2s -- Virginia or Scrub Pine *Pinus virginiana* Mill. **10**

18. Cones 4" to 6" long – Norway Spruce *Picea abies* (L.)
Karst. **16**
18. Cones less than 3" long - 19

8
9
10

11   x 1/2

12

13

14   15

19. Cones purplish at maturity *, scales with evident ragged edges --
    Black Spruce *Picea mariana* (Mill.) B.S.P. **21**
19. Cones brownish at maturity, scale edges smooth or very slightly
    ragged - 20

   20. Cones about ¾" long, or less -- Eastern Hemlock
         Tsuga canadensis (L.) Carr. **19, 20**
   20. Cones more than 1" long - 21

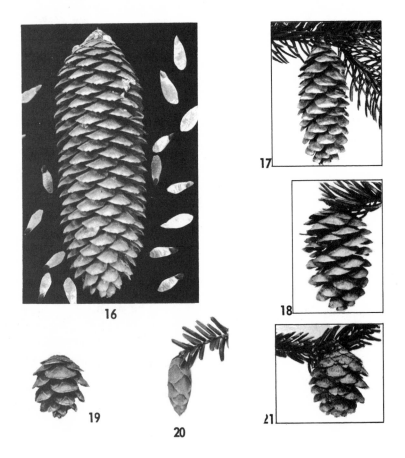

16

17

18

19

20

21

* They lose this color during the winter, but persist on the tree for many
years.

21. Cones oblong, the scales flexible, with smooth straight edges --
White Spruce *Picea glauca* (Moench.) Voss. **17**
21. Cones more ovoid (egg-shaped), scales brittle, with rounded
slightly ragged edges -- Red Spruce *Picea rubens* Sarg. **18**

    22. "Seeds" (nutlets) conspicuously winged (use hand lens),
    cone scales fall away at maturity or during the ensuing
    winter - 23
    22. "Seeds" not conspicuously winged, cone scales
    persistent (look for old cones from previous season) --
    Speckled Alder *Alnus rugosa* (DuRoi) Spreng. **22,** or
    Smooth Alder *Alnus serrulata* (Ait.) Willd.

23. Cone matures in late spring or early summer, and then
falls apart; nutlets with hairy wings (use lens) -- Red or
River Birch *Betula nigra* L. **23, 24, 25**
23. Cone matures in autumn; nutlet wings essentially smooth
(glabrous) - 24

    24. Cone upright on branchlet; short-stalked; oblong;
    scales persistent during part of the winter - - - - - - - - - - 25
    24. Cone pendent, spreading (sideways), or somewhat
    upright; long-stalked; narrowly cylindrical; scales
    usually falling away at maturity - - - - - - - - - - - - - - - - 26

22

23

24   X 3

25   X 3

25. Scales hairy (use lens) -- Yellow Birch *Betula alleghaniensis* Britton (*B. lutea* Michx. F.) **26, 27, 28**
25. Scales essentially glabrous -- Sweet or Black Birch *Betula lenta* L. **29, 30, 31**

    26. Cone pendent, 1" to 1½" long -- Paper or White Birch *Betula papyrifera* Marsh. **32, 33, 34**
    26. Cone spreading or somewhat erect, about ¾" long -- Gray Birch *Betula populifolia* Marsh. **35, 36, 37**

27. Fruit with a thin wing at the end, or encircling the seed cavity - 28
27. Fruit not winged - 44

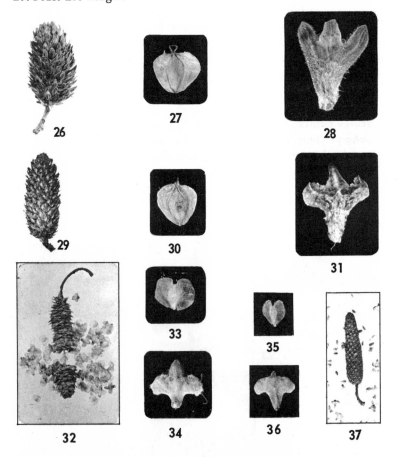

Illustrations with black background all ×3

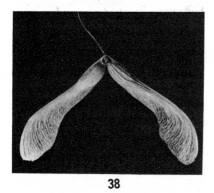

38

39

40

41

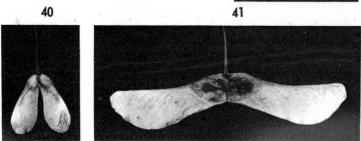

33. Fruits borne in clusters -- Sugar Maple *Acer saccharum* Marsh, **44,** and Black Maple *Acer nigrum* Michx. f.

33. Fruits borne alternately along a central stem - - - - - - - - - - - - 34

    34. Wings about ½'' long; seed portion bright red -- Mountain Maple *Acer spicatum* Lam. **42**

    34. Wings about ¾'' long; seed portion reddish brown -- Striped Maple or Moosewood *Acer pensylvanicum* L. **43**

35. Wing terminal (at end of seed cavity) - - - - - - - - - - - - - - - - 36

35. Wing encircling the seed cavity -40

    36. Fruit a nutlet borne at the base of a 3-lobed wing-like bract (modified leaf); or in one end of a bladder-like sac -- Hornbeams (see No. 100)

    36. Fruit actually winged - 37

37. Seed cavity 4-angled in cross-section -- Tuliptree or Yellow-poplar *Liriodendron tulipifera* L. **45, 46**

37. Seed cavity more or less circular or flattened in cross-section - - 38

    38. Fruit shaped like a lance head or narrow oar blade - - - - - - 39

    38. Fruit wider, somewhat oblong -- Black ash *Fraxinus nigra* Marsh. **49,** and Blue Ash *Fraxinus quadrangulata* Michx. **48**

39. Wing about 3/16'' wide; seed portion moderately tapered (see illustration) - - White Ash *Fraxinus americana* L. **50**

39. Wing about 1/8'' wide; seed portion extremely narrow and tapering (see illustration) -- Green Ash *Fraxinus pennsylvanica* Marsh. **51,** (Formerly red ash was F. *pennsylvanica,* and green ash was F. *penn.* var. *lanceolata.* Red ash is now synonomous with green ash.)

    40. Wing oblong, twisted, resembling a propeller blade -- Ailanthus or Tree-of-heaven *Ailanthus altissima* (Mill.) Swing. **47**

    40. Wing oval to circular - 41

42

43

44

45

46

47

48

49

50

51

41. Fruit about 1'' long, 2-seeded, prominently veined, smooth -- Hop-tree or Wafer-ash *Ptelea trifoliata* L. **56**
41. Fruit usually less than 1'' long, 1-seeded, less prominently veined, hairy (use lens) - 42

     42. Fruit about ½'' long, hairy only along edge of wing -- American Elm *Ulmus americana* L. **54**
     42. Fruit about ¾'' long, hairy over entire surface, or only on seed portion - 43

43. Fruit hairy over entire surface, seed cavity indistinct - - Rock Elm or Cork Elm *Ulmus thomasii* Sarg. **53**
43. Fruit hairy only on seed portion, seed cavity distinct -- Slippery Elm *Ulmus rubra* Muhl. (*U. fulva* Michx.) **52**

     44. Fruit fleshy, shows no signs of splitting along definite seams - 45
     44. Fruit dry, or semi-fleshy, may or may not split open at maturity - 76

45. Fruit made up of many small individual units packed so closely together that one fruit seems to result* - - - - - - - - - - - 46
45. Fruits evidently distinct although they may be close together - 49

52   **53**   X 3   **54**

*If the "fruit" is upright, bright red and four or more inches loₙ̫ᵦ, see No. 54.

55 X 1/2

56 X 1

57

52. Fruit oblong, ridges of pit (nut) sharp -- Butternut
    Juglans cinerea L. **58, 59, 60**
52. Fruit globose, ridges of pit rounded -- Black Walnut
    Juglans nigra L. **61, 62, 63**

53. Fruit clusters attached to a characteristic strap-like bract
    (modified leaf), fruit hard and gray-green -- Basswoods
    Tilia spp. **66**
53. Bract lacking, fruits mostly red, blue, or black - - - - - - - - - - - 54

    54. Fruits 1/8'' to 1/4'' in diameter, fifty or more borne
        closely together in an upright cone-shaped mass - - - - - - - 55
    54. Fruits larger, fewer in number, or borne singly - - - - - - - - 56

58

59

60

61

62

63

55. Each small fruit covered with long sour-tasting glandular
    hairs, "cone" very compact -- Staghorn Sumac *Rhus typhina*
    L. **64**

55. Each fruit covered with short hairs, "cone" more open --
    Smooth Sumac *Rhus glabra* L.

   56. Several bright red fruits borne close together forming
       a head -- Flowering Dogwood *Cornus florida* L. **65**
   56. Fruits conspicuously stalked, or borne singly - - - - - - - - - 57

57. Flesh relatively dry, not juicy - 58
57. Flesh soft, more or less juicy - 59

   58. Fruit borne on a long stalk, flesh with a date-like
       flavor, pit marked something like a golf ball --
       Hackberry *Celtis occidentalis* L. **67, 68**
   58. Fruit short-stalked or sessile (stalk lacking,), flesh
       aromatic, pit not marked as above -- Eastern Redcedar
       (see No. 4)

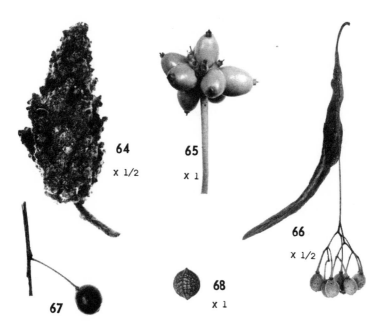

64
x 1/2

65
x 1

66
x 1/2

67

68
x 1

59. Fruit borne erect on a bright red club-shaped stalk, -- Sassafras
    Sassafras albidum (Nutt.) Nees. **69**
59. Fruit borne in drooping or spreading clusters, paired or
    solitary - 60

    60. Fruit red to black, or yellowish - - - - - - - - - - - - - - - - 61
    60. Fruit dark blue - 64

61. Fruit cluster a raceme (fruits borne on short side stalks
    attached to a central stem) - 62
61. Fruits borne on long stalks attached to twig - - - - - - - - - - - - 63

    62. Fruits with a strong wine flavor -- Black Cherry
         Prunus serotina Ehrh. **71**
    62. Fruits extremely puckery -- Choke Cherry *Prunus
         virginiana* L.

63. Fruit about ¼" in diameter, bright red, sour -- Fire Cherry or
    Pin Cherry *Prunus pensylvanica* L.
63. Fruit larger, yellow to dark red -- Other Cherries and Plums
    (the latter usually larger) *Prunus* spp.

    64. Fruits commonly borne in pairs (may be solitary or in
         3s) at the end of a long slender stalk; pit ribbed - - Black
         Tupelo or Blackgum *Nyssa sylvatica* Marsh. **72**
    64. Fruits borne in clusters of several to many; pit not
         ribbed - 65

65. Pit short-ovoid (egg-shaped), grooved - - Alternate-leaf
    or Pagoda Dogwood *Cornus alternifolia* L. f.
65. Pit flattened, not grooved -- Nannyberry *Viburnum lentago*
    L. and Blackhaw *Viburnum prunifolium* L.

    66. Flesh hard or mealy, not soft when ripe - - - - - - - - - - - - 67
    66. Flesh soft, usually juicy - 68

67. Fruit bluish, cone scales visible with a lens (a conifer)
    Redcedar (See No. 4)
67. Fruit bright red, not a cone (a broadleaved evergreen)
    American Holly *Ilex opaca* Ait. **70**

68. Fruit a large berry with scattered seeds which are
½" or more in length - 69
68. Fruit a pome (like an apple); or small with seeds
¼" or less in length - 70

69. Fruit globose with a conspicuous persistent woody calyx at
the base; seeds flattened - - Persimmon *Diospyros virginiana*
L. **73, 74**
69. Fruit oblong, lacking a calyx, seeds ovoid - - Pawpaw *Asimina
triloba* (L.) Dunal

70. Fruit a pome -71
70. Fruit not a pome. black, flesh has strong cascara taste --
European Buckthorn *Rhamnus cathartica* L.

71. Fruit large, mostly 1" or more in diameter - - - - - - - - - - - - - 72
71. Fruit small, less than 1" in diameter - - - - - - - - - - - - - - - - 74

72. Grit cells present -- Pear *Pyrus communis* L.
72. Grit cells lacking - 73

70 X 1/2

69

73

72

71
X 1/2

74

73. Fruit stalk long and slender; fruit fragrant -- Sweet Crab
Apple *Malus coronaria* (L.) Mill.
73. Fruit stalk short and stout; fruit but slightly fragrant --
Apple *Malus pumila* Mill.

    74. Fruits purplish, ripening in June or July - - Serviceberry
      or Shadbush *Amelanchier* spp.
    74. Fruits bright red; ripening in autumn - - - - - - - - - - - - - - 75

75. Fruits many in a cluster -- Mountain-ash *Sorbus* spp. **75**
75. Fruits few in a cluster or solitary -- Hawthorn or Thornapple
Crataegus spp. **76**

    76. Fruit made up of many small units packed tightly
      together (compound) - 77
    76. Fruit solitary, or borne in loose clusters - - - - - - - - - - - - 80

77. Fruit cone-shaped, upright, semi-fleshy (Magnolias) - - - - - - - - 78
77. Fruit globose, pendent, dry - 79

    78. Fruit oblong, 2" to 3" long — Cucumbertree *Magnolia*
      acuminata L. **77**
    78. Fruit oval, about 2" long -- Sweetbay *Magnolia*
      virginiana L.

79. Each beaked unit (capsule) splits along two seams - - Sweetgum
or Redgum *Liquidambar styraciflua* L. **78**
79. Each unit a small dry somewhat angled achene bearing a
spine at the tip and a circle of hairs at the base, falling
away from the core during the winter -- American Sycamore
or Planetree *Platanus occidentalis* L. **79, 80**

    80. Fruit an acorn (see Page 37) - - - - - - - - - - - - - - - - - - - 81
    80. Fruit not an acorn - 97

81. Inside of shell of nut not velvety; seed relatively sweet
(White Oaks) - 82
81. Inside of shell of nut with a velvet-like lining; seed
extremely bitter and puckery (Red Oaks) - - - - - - - - - - - - - - 87

X 1

75

76

77

78

X 1

79 X 1

80

82. Acorn borne on a stalk 1½" to 3" long - - Swamp White
     Oak *Quercus bicolor* Willd. **84**
82. Acorn short-stalked, or sessile (no stalk) - - - - - - - - - - - - 83

83. Acorn cup with a conspicuous fringe — Bur Oak
    Quercus macrocarpa Michx. **81**
83. Acorn cup not fringed - 84

    84. Cup scales swollen giving them a warty appearance --
         White Oak *Quercus alba* L. **82**
    84. Cup scales flat or nearly so - - - - - - - - - - - - - - - - - - - 85

85. Inner surface of cup tending to be straight from rim to bottom,
    acorn about 1" long Chestnut Oak *Quercus prinus* L. (*Q.
    montana* Willd.) **85, 86**
85. Inner surface of cup curved from rim to bottom, acorn usually
    less than 1" long - 86

    86. Nut tawny, often hairy at the tip - - Post Oak *Quercus
         stellata* Wangenh. **83**
    86. Nut brown to black, smooth -- Chinkapin Oak *Quercus
        muehlenbergii* Engelm. **87**

87. Cup saucer-shaped, enclosing the nut only at the base - - - - - - 88
87. Cup bowl- or top-shaped, enclosing one third or more of
    the nut - 90

    88. Acorn about 1" long -- Northern Red Oak *Quercus
         rubra* L. (*Q. borealis* Michx.) * **88, 89**
    88. Acorn about ½" long - 89

89. Cup scales reddish brown -- Pin Oak *Quercus palustris*
    Muenchh. **90**
89. Cup scales greenish brown - Willow Oak *Quercus phellos*
    L. **91, 92**

*Note variation in acorn shape. Number **88** is the usual form in
Northeastern U.S.

90. Acorn about 1" long -91
90. Acorn less than 1" long - 92

91. Cup scales tightly appressed, often appearing varnished; concentric rings commonly present around tip of acorn -- Scarlet Oak *Quercus coccinea* Muenchh. **93, 94**
91. Cup scales not appressed, dull, not shiny; concentric rings lacking -- Northern Red Oak *Quercus rubra* L. (*Q. borealis* Michx.) **89**

The above illustrations are at approximately natural size.

92. Cup scales tightly appressed, often shiny; concentric
    rings commonly present around tip of acorn -- Scarlet
    Oak *Quercus coccinea* Muenchh. **93, 94**
92. Cup scales not appressed, dull, rings lacking - - - - - - - - - **93**

93. Nut narrowly elliptical or oblong - - - - - - - - - - - - - - - - - - - **94**
93. Nut wider, egg-shaped (ovoid) to hemispherical - - - - - - - - - - - **95**

94. Nut narrowly elliptical, cup thin, the scales appearing
    somewhat fused -- Northern Pin Oak or Jack Oak
    Quercus ellipsoidalis E. J. Hill. **95**
94. Nut oblong with a conspicuous spiked tip, cup thick, the
    scales coarse, conspicuous, rusty-wooly -- Blackjack Oak
    Quercus marilandica Muenchh. **96**

95. Nut somewhat hemispherical; cup scales greenish -- Shingle
    Oak *Quercus imbricaria* Michx. **97**
95. Nut longer than wide; cup scales reddish to gray - - - - - - - - - - **96**

96. Cup sharply constricted at the base -- Bear, or Scrub
    Oak *Quercus ilicifolia* Wangenh. **98**
96. Cup not sharply constricted at the base Black Oak
    Quercus velutina Lam. **99, 100**

97. Fruit a bony or leathery nut, partially or wholly enclosed by
    a husk or sac - **98**
97. Fruit a legume (flat pod), or capsule, in any case at maturity
    splitting along definite seams or sutures - - - - - - - - - - - - - - - -**110**

98. Nutlet small, about ¼" in diameter, or length - - - - - - - - - **99**
98. Nut ½" or more in length - **101**

99. Nutlet globose, with a gray-green wooly outer surface (actually
    drupe-like) (Basswoods, No. 53)
99. Nutlet ovoid (egg-shaped), smooth, either enclosed in a
    papery sac, or borne at the base of a 3-lobed bract - - - - - - - - **100**

100. Nutlet borne enclosed at the base of a papery
     sac -- Hophornbeam *Ostrya virginiana* (Mill.)
     K. Koch **101, 102**
100. Nutlet borne exposed at the base of a 3-lobed
     bract -- American Hornbeam or Bluebeech
     Carpinus caroliniana Walt. **103**

101. Husk does not split at maturity (Walnuts, No. 52.)
101. Husk splits along definite seams or sutures - - - - - - - - - - - 102

    102. Nut leathery and encased in a prickly husk
     (bur)* - 103
    102. Nut bony, encased in a smooth husk
     (Hickories) - 104

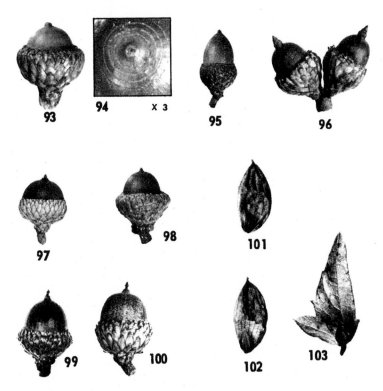

93   94   X 3   95   96

97   98   101

99   100   102   103

Except as noted, the above illustrations are at approximately natural
size.
*See also No. 116

103. Nut rounded in cross-section; spines of bur branched, needle-sharp - - American Chestnut (see note at bottom of page) *Castanea dentata* (Marsh.) Borkh*. **104**

103. Nut triangular in cross-section, spines weak not branched American Beech *Fagus grandifolia* Ehrh. **107, 108**

    104. Husk ¼" or more in thickness - - - - - - - - - - - - - - - - 105
    104. Husk 1/8" or less in thickness - - - - - - - - - - - - - - 107

105. Nut flattened, yellowish to nearly white - - - - - - - - - - - - - -106

105. Nut usually not flattened, brownish in color - - - Mockernut Hickory *Carya tomentosa* Nutt. **105, 106**

    106. Nut 4-ribbed, often rounded at the base -- Shagbark Hickory *Carya ovata* (Mill.) K. Koch **109, 112**
    106. Nut 4-to-6-ribbed, usually pointed at both ends -- Shellbark Hickory *Carya laciniosa* (Michx. f.) Loud. **115**
    (The above features often fail to separate the fruit of these two species.)

107. Nut conspicuously 4-angled (Mockernut, see No. 105).

107. Nut rounded, or inconspicuously angled - - - - - - - - - - - - - 108

    108. Husk winged at the sutures (seams) Bitternut Hickory *Carya cordiformis* (Wangenh.) K. Koch **110, 111**
    108. Husk not winged, either smooth or slightly ridged along the sutures - 109

109. Husk splitting cleanly to the base of the nut -- Red, or Oval Pignut Hickory *Carya ovalis* (Wangenh.) Sarg. **113** and its several varieties.**

109. Husk splitting only about half-way from apex to base, often scarcely opening at all - - Pignut Hickory *Carya glabra* (Mill.) Sweet **114**

*The fruit of the buckeyes and horsechestnut may appear to be a nut answering this description. In reality these fruits are capsules. (See No. 116).

**The 1953 "Check List" makes this species synonomous with *Carya glabra*.

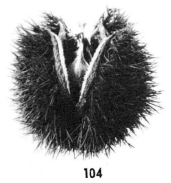

104

105

106

107

108

109

110

111

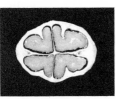

112

113

114

115

110. Fruit a flat pod (legume) -------------------- 111
110. Fruit a capsule, not flat -------------------- 114

111. Pod curved, with irregular wavy edges, often twisted, 8"
or more in length -- Honeylocust *Gleditsia triacanthos*
L. **118**
111. Pod nearly straight, edges not wavy, not twisted, mostly
less than 8" in length ----------------------- 112

    112. Pod heavy and woody, seeds large, about ½" long --
    Kentucky Coffeetree *Gymnocladus dioicus* (L.) K.
    Koch **121**
    112. Pod light, with thin walls, seeds small, ¼" or less
    in length ----------------------------- 113

113. Pod rounded or abruptly pointed at the ends, seeds reniform
(kidney-shaped) Black Locust *Robinia pseudoacacia* L. **116**
113. Pod gradually tapering at the ends, seeds rounded, not
reniform -- Eastern Redbud or Judas-tree *Cercis canadensis*
L. **117**

    114. Capsule globose, 1" or more in diameter --------- 115
    114. Capsule long and cylindrical, or small, less than
    ½" in diameter ------------------------- 117

115. Capsule spiny ----------------------------- 116
115. Capsule essentially smooth, occasionally with warts, or
slight spine-like projections -- Yellow Buckeye *Aesculus
octandra* Marsh. **119, 120**

    116. Spines large, about ¼" long -- Horsechestnut *Aesculus
    hippocastanum* L.
    116. Spines small, about 1/8" or less in length - - Ohio
    Buckeye *Aesculus glabra* Willd.

117. Capsules very small, and filled with tightly packed white
cottony floss some of which is attached to the few seeds - - - 118
117. Capsules do not contain white floss --------------- 121

116

119

120

117

X 2/3

118

X 2/3

121

X 1/2

118. Fruit smooth at the base with no indication of an
     encircling ridge (edge of cup-shaped disk) -- Willows
     Salix spp. **123, 124**
118. Fruit borne in a cup-shaped disk, the edge of which
     may be seen near the base of the capsule (use lens)
     Poplars - 119

119. Capsule thin-walled, narrow and tapering -- Quaking Aspen
     Populus tremuloides Michx. and Bigtooth Aspen *Populus
     grandidentata* Michx.
119. Capsule thick-walled, more or less globose or bead-
     shaped - 120

   120. Capsule opens at 2 sutures (seams) -- Balsam Poplar
        Populus balsamifera L. (*P. tacamahaca* Mill.) **129**
   120. Capsule opens at 3 or 4 sutures -- Eastern Cotton-
        wood *Populus deltoides* Bartr. **127**

121. Capsules 6" or more in length; seeds bearded at the ends
     -- Catalpa *Catalpa* spp. **122, 125**
121. Capsules less than 1" long - - - - - - - - - - - - - - - - - - 122

   122. Capsules with heavy, woody walls; seeds large,
        shiny, black -- Witch-hazel *Hamamelis virginiana*
        L. **126**
   122. Capsules with thin papery walls, or somewhat
        fleshy - 123

123. Capsule reddish, somewhat fleshy, strongly lemon-scented;
     seeds large (3/16") Common Prickly-ash *Zanthoxylum
     americanum* Mill.
123. Capsule yellowish or brownish; seeds extremely small
     (almost like dust) - 124

   124. Capsule nearly globose -- Mountain-laurel *Kalmia
        latifolia* L.
   124. Capsule oblong - conical - - - - - - - - - - - - - - - - - 125

125. Capsule covered with minute sticky hairs -- Rosebay Rhodo-
     dendron or Great Rhododendron *Rhododendron maximum*
     L. **128**
125. Capsule smooth -- Sourwood *Oxydendrum arboreum* DC.

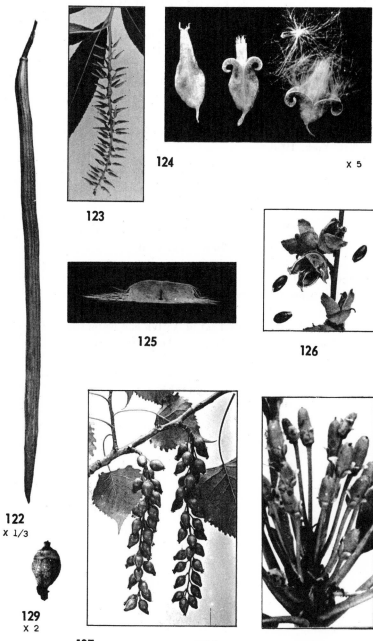

123

124 X 5

125

126

122
X 1/3

129
X 2

127 X 2/3 **128**

SELECTED REFERENCES

1. Blakeslee, A.F. and C.D. Jarvis. New England Trees in Winter Bul. No. 69, Storrs Agri. Exp. Sta. Storrs. Conn. 1911.

2. Brown H.P. Trees of Northeastern United States. Christopher Pub. Co., Boston, Mass. 1938.

3. Fernald, M. L. Gray's Manual of Botany. 8th Ed. Amer. Book Co., New York. 1950.

4. Harlow, W. M. Trees of the Eastern and Central United States and Canada. Dover Publications, New York, 1957.

5. _____ _____ and E.S. Harrar. Textbook of Dendrology. McGraw-Hill Book Co., New York. 1950.

6. Hough. R.B. Trees of the Northern States and Canada Pub. by author. Lowville, New York. 1907.

7. Little, E.L., Jr. Check List of Native and Naturalized Trees of the United States. U.S. Dept. of Agri., Wash., D.C. 1953.

NOTES

INDEX TO COMMON NAMES

Twig and Buds of Black Maple
(Enlarged about 8 diameters)

Twig Key to the Deciduous Woody Plants
of
Eastern North America

By
WILLIAM M. HARLOW, PH. D.
Professor of Wood Technology

State University of New York
College of Forestry
Syracuse, New York

Fourth Revised Edition

Dover Publications, Inc.

PREFACE TO THE FIRST EDITION

Several keys to deciduous woody plants in winter are accessible to students, but to the author's knowledge none of these is accompanied by photographic halftones of buds and twigs. For this reason, it has seemed advisable to prepare such a key using small "inset" illustrations. These permit of a visual check of the subject matter included in the key and at the same time make the key more readily usable, and more accurate in identification, especially to the novice in this field.

In preparing the key, William Trelease's "Winter Botany" has been invaluable, and deserves to be known by all those interested in woody plants. "New England Trees in Winter" by Blakeslee and Jarvis has also been freely consulted as well as the other texts listed under "Selected References."

PREFACE TO THE FOURTH EDITION

The illustrations have in most cases been doubled in size (now 3×) and it is hoped they will display greater detail than previously. Since the U. S. Forest Service now uses the International Rules, appropriate changes in nomenclature have been made. Suggestions for improving The Key are always welcome.

Common and scientific tree names in this printing are from the 1953 U. S. Forest Service Check List. Scientific names of shrubs are from Gray's Manual, 8th Ed., and shrub common names follow Standardized Plant Names.

Syracuse, N. Y.
Nov. 1954

William M. Harlow

INTRODUCTION

To most otherwise "forest-minded" folk, the approach of autumn with its showers of many-colored leaves, spells the end of the season's activities in the indentification of deciduous trees and shrubs. Without leaves, the members of the forest community, unless they be relatively large, seem to lose much of their summer's identity and may even descend to the level of "brush." This is in reality not the case, as may be easily discovered by examining any leafless twig with a 10-× pocket lens, or even with the naked eye. A casual glance at Plate I will also serve to show that woody plants in winter are anything but featureless.

The first section comprises a description of some prominent twig characters of value in identification. At this point it should perhaps be mentioned that these so-called "winter features" are safe guides for a much longer period, and that twig and bud characters are in fact usable over the entire year except for three to four months in late spring and early summer when most of the growth for the current year takes place. In this connection, the winter buds of most deciduous trees and shrubs are already sufficiently formed for purposes of identification by July or early August.

The accompanying key does not permit of identification to species of all woody plants of Eastern North America.[1] In a number of instances it has seemed inadvisable at present to proceed further than groups of species since the twig characters of closely allied forms are often very similar, and their inclusion would make the key unwieldy as well as difficult to use by the beginner. Several of the typically Southwestern legumes have been omitted as have also a few of the less common shrubs. Although restricted principally to native forms, a few of the commoner ornamental, or naturalized species have been listed.

THE STRUCTURAL FEATURES OF BUDS AND TWIGS

Buds

These structures which are plainly visible on most twigs are indicative of a resting stage brought on presumably by climatic conditions unfavorable to continued growth. A bud is in reality an em-

---

[1] For the most part coincides with the area covered by Gray's "New Manual of Botany."

bryonic branch and as such bears a number of miniature leaves or
flowers which in many cases (as in yellow-poplar) are clearly recog-
nizable when the bud is carefully dissected.[1] The buds of most
woody plants are provided with scales, but in a few forms the buds
are unprotected except for the first pair of leaves which curl inward
and shield those beneath (Plate I, Fig. 4). Buds of this sort are said
to be *naked* in contrast to the more common *scaly* type which exhi-
bits one or more scales (Fig. 1). Certain woody plants seem to lack
buds; in such instances, however, they are usually embedded in the
twig and emerge when growth begins in the spring (Figs. 5 and 12).

A marked difference in the size and form of individual buds is
often observable on the same twig; the larger ones frequently prove
to be *flower buds*, since they contain the rudiments of flowers, while
the smaller and usually more numerous buds enclose only embryonic
leaves, — *leaf buds*: (Figs. 2 and 3 respectively). In some species,
mixed buds containing both flowers and leaves are found.

The normal position for buds is either in the axil or upper angle
between leaf and stem, or at the apex (tip) of a twig. Those occurring
in the leaf axils are called *lateral* or *axillary* buds, while the word
terminal is reserved for the apical bud which is usually larger. This,
as the term implies, is always borne directly on the end of the twig
and when once formed limits any further growth in length for the season.[2] The twigs of some species lack a true terminal bud, and the
growing point continues to advance until it exhausts the readily
available food supply or is affected adversely by some other factor.
The tender growing shoot then wilts and dies back to the last well
formed lateral which meanwhile assumes a more or less terminal position (even though it often slants); this lateral bud is called a false
or *pseudo-terminal* bud. A portion of the dead branch tip may persist
for some time (Fig. 10) or the withered shoot may slough off, leaving
a *branch scar* (Fig. 13). This never shows bundle scars, but rather
three concentric rings of bark, wood, and pith respectively; it should
not be confused with the leaf scar (see under leaf and bundle scars),
which occurs on the opposite side of the twig directly below the
pseudo-terminal bud. It is often very important to determine whether

[1] Although the twigs of many species can be identified with the naked
eye, a pocket magnifier (hand lens) which enlarges five to ten times is always a help, and often a necessity for seeing the finer details of twig
structure.

[2] Sometimes the terminal bud, and also the laterals, which usually open the following spring, become active later in the same season in which they were formed,
and so-called "secondary growth" in length takes place. This is especially common
in sprouts from a new stump.

a twig has the one or the other type of end bud: a true terminal bud is usually larger than the laterals; and the twig never shows a branch scar at the base of the bud.

Three types of arrangement of lateral buds are found on twigs, viz: (1) *whorled* — in threes (or more), all at about the same height on the twig; (2) *opposite* — in pairs, opposite to each other (Fig. 9); and (3) *alternate* — in more or less evident spirals, with one bud at each node (Figs. 6 and 11). In all three of these arrangements, each bud is inserted directly above a leaf scar (Fig. 7). In some woody plants, there is more than one axillary bud at a node, and the "extra" bud or buds are then designated as *accessory*. Two kinds of accessory buds are recognized, viz: (1) those which occur on either side of the normal lateral bud, the *collaterals* (Fig. 8), and (2) those inserted above the lateral bud, which are said to be *superposed* (Fig. 7).

A few woody plants are featured by buds with a single caplike cover scale which usually splits along the side next to the twig when the bud opens. This condition is relatively rare, however, and most buds are covered with from two to many scales, the number being practically constant for a given species or group of species. If the scales meet exactly without any overlapping (Fig. 3), they are said to be *valvate*, while the term *imbricate* indicates the more usual condition in which the scales do overlap (Fig. 1).

Leaf Scars and Bundle Scars

Some time prior to leaf fall, there develops at the base of the leaf stem (petiole), a protective abscission layer consisting of cells which are more or less corky next to the twig, and thin walled and somewhat loosely organized toward the leaf. Slowly, the communication between leaf and twig lessens until finally the petiole becomes so weakened at the absciss layer that the leaf falls off and only the corky place of attachment (now the *leaf scar*), (Figs. 4, 5, and 7) is left to mark its previous position. Leaf fall is a revolutionary change for the tree to undergo and marks the beginning of the resting stage which characterizes deciduous trees during the winter months.

PLATE I

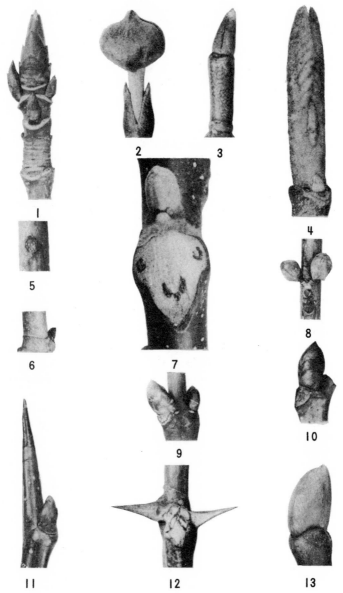

Description of Plate I[1]

Fig. 1.   Twig and buds of sugar maple showing bud scale scars.

Fig. 2.   Flower bud of flowering dogwood.

Fig. 3.   Leaf bud of flowering dogwood showing valvate scales.

Fig. 4.   Naked bud of wayfaring tree.

Fig. 5.   The leaf scar covers the bud in fragrant sumac.

Fig. 6.   Stipule scars appearing as a line encircling the twig of sycamore.

Fig. 7.   Twig and buds of butternut showing a leaf scar, bundle scars, and superposed buds.

Fig. 8.   Collateral flower buds of spicebush: the smaller pointed bud in the center is the axillary, or lateral leaf bud.

Fig. 9.   Leaf scar and stipule scars of bladdernut.

Fig. 10. Pseudo-terminal bud and branch stub (right) of red mulberry.

Fig. 11. A thorn (pear).

Fig. 12. Stipular spines of black locust. This also shows the absence of visible buds. The buds are embedded beneath the leaf scar and emerge when growth is resumed.

Fig. 13. Pseudo-terminal bud and branch scar of basswood. The leaf scar is on the other side of the twig.

[1]Photographs reproduced at about four times natural size.

On the surface of the leaf scar may be found from one to many small dots or lines, the *bundle scars,* which indicate where the channels of sap conduction entered or passed from the leaf to the stem (Figs. 4. 5, and 7). They present a variety of patterns and although often difficult to see without a lens, are of considerable diagnostic value. Occasionally, the bundle scars may be indistinct or they may be obscured by a portion of the leaf base which persists on the twig. In such instances a better view may often be obtained by carefully slicing off the surface layer of the leaf scar with a razor blade.

Stipule Scars

Stipules are small leaf-like organs occurring in pairs on the twig, one at each side of the petiole. They generally fall during the summer (rarely persistent), and usually leave on the twig small narrow scars (Fig. 9), which in some species completely encircle it (Fig. 6). *Stipule scars* are not found in certain groups and, therefore, their presence or absence is often of value in identification.

Bud Scale Scars

These are narrow scars left by the scales of the terminal bud of the previous season, and appear as short, closely spaced transverse lines (Fig. 1). *Bud scale* scars are useful in determining the age of a twig since they persist for a number of years until obliterated as the bark thickens. Each group of scars indicates the end of a season's growth. The twig illustrated in Fig. 1 made very slow growth during its last season.

Fruit Scars

These are similar in appearance to branch scars, but are often found in a terminal position. In twigs which normally have true terminal buds, their presence may be misleading unless a non-fruiting twig can be found.

Thorns and Spines

Both of these structures appear as sharp outgrowths of the twig, but presumably have different origins. *Thorns* are modified branches and as such usually bear leaf scars (Fig. 11), or are themselves branched. *Spines* are considered to be modified persistent stipules (Fig. 12), or modified leaf blades; or they may arise from the cortical tissues beneath the epidermis.

Spur Shoots

In some species, certain twigs (often but not always twigs heavily shaded) grow very slowly but at the same time maintain a more or less normal number of leaves. This results in short, usually stocky spurs with crowded leaf scars, termed spur shoots. Apple, cherry, and birch trees are among those characterized by dwarfed branchlets of this type.

Lenticels

Lenticels are small, often wart-like dots or patches distributed over the surface of the twig, and serve to admit air into the tissues beneath (Fig. 7).

Twig Surfaces, and Shapes in Cross Section

Twigs may be smooth (glabrous), hairy (pubescent), or covered with a bloom (glaucous): They may appear polished or dull. In cross-section, twigs are circular (terete) oval, or from three to five angled.

Composition and Shape of the Pith

Pith features are often very striking, and are especially useful in twig identification. In examining a twig, a smooth lengthwise cut should be made through the center with a razor blade or sharp knife.

As seen in such a lengthwise section, pith is commonly *continuous* and *homogeneous*, i. e. appears to be of uniform structure throughout (Plate II, Fig. 1). However, in some species (yellow-poplar), the whitish pith context is interrupted at intervals by narrow bars of darker tissue, and since these appear as cross partitions, the pith is said

to be *diaphragmed* (Fig. 2). Pith is sometimes spongy, i. e., filled
with minute irregular cavities (Fig. 3), and occasionally *chambered*,
i. e., hollow except for transverse partitions (Fig. 4). Rarely it is
partially or entirely excavated, or lacking.

The shape of the pith in transverse section is often characteristic;
it may be terete (Fig. 5), oval, triangular (Fig. 7), 5-angled or star-
shaped (Fig. 6). If available, a drop of phloroglucin reagent, or even
dilute fountain pen ink will bring out the outline of the pith.

Types of Pith

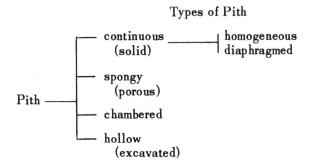

PLATE II

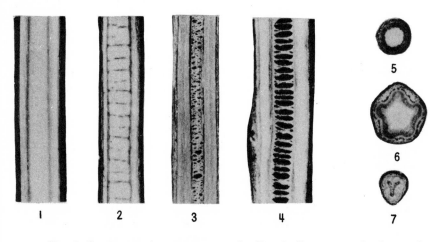

Fig. 1. Continuous, homogeneous pith. Fig. 2. Continuous, diaphragmed
pith. Fig. 3. Spongy pith. Fig. 4. Chambered pith. Figs. 5, 6, and 7 indicate variations in shape in cross-section: (5) terete or circular; (6) angled
or star-shaped; (7) triangular.

How to Use the Key

Before attempting to identify a twig, compare it carefully with the description and illustrations given for poison-ivy and poison-sumac on the next page. These plants are poisonous to the touch and are dangerous to handle in winter as well as in summer. If possible find out whether the twig was collected from a tree, a shrub, or a vine (see definitions in the glossary); also if spines, thorns, or spur shoots were present even though they do not show on the twig collected. If choosing material directly, collect several twigs of moderate growth, avoiding those of very slow or fast growth, respectively, since these are often not typical. Especially avoid young stump sprouts on account of their probable departure from the normal, even though in some instances they may be correctly identified with the key.

Having observed these points, suppose that the twig shown in Fig. 1, Plate I has been chosen (although this represents very slow growth). In approaching the key, it will be noticed that there are always two alternatives presented for consideration, only one of which should fit the twig in question. Starting with No. 1 in the key, it will be evident that the leaf scars and buds are opposite. This takes one to No. 2. The bundle scars are three in number, hence the second part of No. 2 is followed to No. 12. Stipule scars are lacking, and the second part of No. 12 is followed to No. 13. Bundle scars are again three rather than numerous, therefore the second part of No. 13 takes the reader to No. 16. The buds are clearly visible, which brings one to No. 17. The buds are obviously scaly and therefore No. 19 is consulted. The leaf scars are narrow and V or U-shaped which directs the search to No. 24. There is more than one scale, and hence one arrives by elimination at No. 26. The scales are imbricate and this brings one to No. 36. The buds are not blue or purplish, and the sap is clear, so No. 38 presents itself for consideration. The buds are brown to black which leads one to No. 39, and since thorns are never present and the buds are opposite, No. 40 is scrutinized. The twig is somewhat shiny with only moderately prominent lenticels and by comparing it with illustrations 36 and 37, it is evident that the twig is that of sugar maple, rather than black maple.

On page 34, No. 124 will be found reading Shadbush *Amelanchier* spp. "spp." is the plural of the word species abbreviated. It signifies that there are two or more species which the Key does not attempt to separate.

Poison-ivy *Toxicodendron radicans* (L.)
Kuntze

The twigs and naked buds are brownish, and
the leaf scars V- or U-shaped with several
bundle scars; the lenticels are usually conspicuous. This species is among the common-
est of roadside plants over a considerable
portion of its range. It is usually a vine, either
prostrate upon the ground or climbing, but may
sometimes appear shrubby, especially when cut
repeatedly. The fruit is white or ivory, and is
born in open, drooping clusters which persist
to some extent during the winter.

1

Poison-sumac *Toxicodendron vernix* (L.)
Kuntze

The twigs are moderately stout, yellowish
brown, and rather conspicuously mottled. The
terminal bud is broadly conical with somewhat
hairy scales. The leaf scars are shield shaped
with a number of scattered bundle scars. This
species is usually restricted to swamps where
it is often exceedingly common. The fruit is
similar in appearance to that of poison-ivy, but
is borne on longer more drooping stems.

Poison-oak *Toxicodendron quercifolium* (Michx.)
Greene

The twigs are similar to those of poison-ivy,
but the habit is more shrubby.

2

All three species have alternate leaf scars.

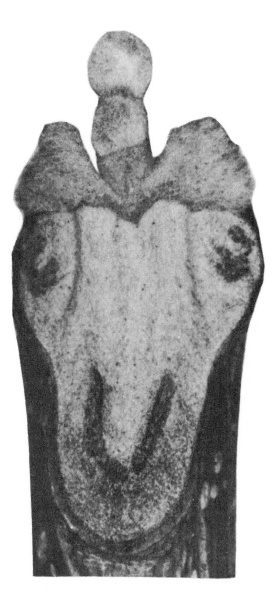

Leaf Scar of Butternut
(Enlarged about 10×)

THE KEY[1]

1. Leaf scars opposite, sub-opposite, or whorled - - - - - - - - - - - 2
1. Leaf scars or buds alternate - 45

    2. Bundle scar one, appearing as a dot, straight line,
       crescent, or U-shaped - 3
    2. Bundle scars 3 or more, sometimes numerous and close
       together in an open or closed ellipse - - - - - - - - - - - - - 12

3. Woody vines -. 4
3. Shrubby or arborescent - 6

    4. Stems 6- to 12-angled; petiole fragments usually persistent;
       pith continuous. Clematis *Clematis* spp. 1
    4. Stems usually circular in cross-section; leaf scars present;
       petioles deciduous; pith spongy or hollow - - - - - - - - - 5

5. End section of stem shows a maltese cross-shaped pattern;
   pith usually spongy, eventually hollow. Crossvine *Bignonia*
   capreolata L. 2
5. End section lacking a cross; aerial roots often present;
   surface of twig often warty; pith spongy, sometimes incompletely excavated. Trumpetcreeper *Campsis radicans* (L.)
   Seem. 3

    6. Leaf scars nearly circular; stipules persistent, or their
       scars nearly connecting the leaf scars; bundle scars
       crescent or U-shaped. Buttonbush *Cephalanthus occi-*
       dentalis L. 4
    6. Leaf scars half round, semi-elliptical, or shield shaped;
       stipule scars lacking or very indistinct - - - - - - - - - - - - 7

7. Leaf scars small and inconspicuous, usually torn; bundle
   scars dot-like, or indistinct; pith very small,[2] continuous,
   or hollow - 8
7. Leaf scars readily distinguishable, bundle scar a straight
   or curved line, or U-shaped - 9

    8. Pith hollow. Snowberry *Symphoricarpos albus* (L.) Blake
    8. Pith continuous. Indiancurrant *Symphoricarpos orbiculatus*
       Moench 5

[1] All illustrations are at a magnification of 3 diameters unless otherwise indicated.

[2] If twigs are covered with chaff-like red-brown scales — it is Buffalo-berry *Shepherdia canadensis* (L.) Nutt.

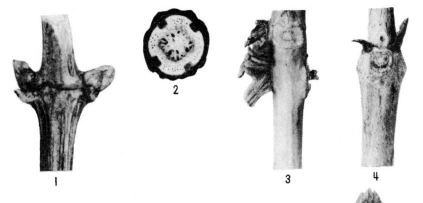

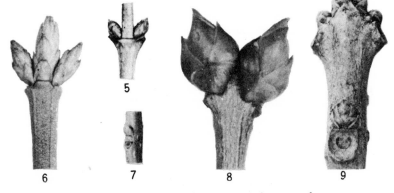

9. Pith spongy, finally incompletely excavated, somewhat
   greenish; stipule scars minute; often indistinct; twigs sometimes with corky wings or ridges. Spindletree, Burningbush
   Euonymus spp. 6
9. Pith continuous, white; stipule scars lacking; twigs not
   corky - 10

  10. Leaf scars and buds very small, the latter superposed;
      twigs slender, sometimes thorny. Swamp-privet
      Forestiera acuminata (Michx.) Poir. 7
  10. Leaf scars and buds moderately large; superposed buds
      present or lacking; twigs never thorny - - - - - - - - - - - - 11

11. Lenticels not conspicuously warty, collateral buds often
    present. Common Lilac *Syringa vulgaris* L. 8
11. Lenticels warty; superposed buds sometimes present.
    Fringetree *Chionanthus virginicus* L. 9

12. Stipule scars prominent (not connected), elongated or half round[1]; terminal bud lacking; bark on older twigs green with white markings. Bladdernut *Staphylea trifolia* L. 10

12. Stipule scars lacking; terminal bud present or lacking (if stipule scars seem to be present, and the pith is very large, see No. 22) - 13

13. Bundle scars numerous, close together, forming an oval, ellipse, or crescent-shaped pattern, open or nearly closed at the top - 14

13. Bundle scars 3 to 7, not as above, sometimes in three groups - 16

14. Terminal bud present (see separate key to species, page 47).

14. Terminal bud lacking - 15

15. Pith chambered or sometimes hollow; superposed buds usually present. Royal Paulownia, or Empresstree *Paulownia tomentosa* (Thunb.) Sieb. and Zucc. 11

15. Pith continuous; lateral buds solitary. Catalpa *Catalpa* spp. 12

16. Buds partially or entirely hidden beneath the membranous leaf scar; bundle scars horseshoe shaped, or appearing as a hoof print.[2] Mockorange *Philadelphus* spp. 13

16. Buds visible; bundle scars not as above - - - - - - - - - - 17

17. Buds naked - 18

17. Buds scaly - 19

18. Buds gray. Wayfaringtree *Viburnum lantana* L.

18. Buds reddish brown (rusty). Hobblebush *Viburnum alnifolium* Marsh. Flower bud 14 Leaf bud 15

19. Leaf scars broad and conspicuous - - - - - - - - - - - - - - - 20

19. Leaf scars narrow and V- or U-shaped, or small and inconspicuous - 24

20. Pith occupying a large portion of the first year's twig - 21

20. Pith moderate in size - 23

[1]Lines or wrinkles in the bark connecting the leaf scars should not be mistaken for stipule scars.

[2]If the twigs are slender or purplish or reddish, see also the dogwoods, Nos. 32 to 35.

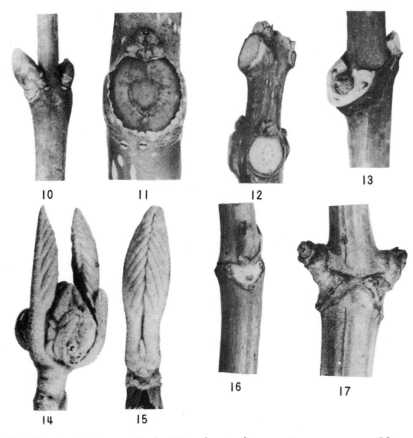

10   11   12

13

14   15

16

17

21. Terminal bud usually lacking; lenticels conspicuous - - - - - 22
21. Terminal bud often present; lenticels inconspicuous, or
    lacking. Hydrangea *Hydrangea* spp. (Also No. 43) 16

    22. Pith white; buds medium sized; conical and somewhat
        depressed. American or Common Elder *Sambucus cana-*
        densis L. 17
    22. Pith salmon colored; buds large and ovoid. Red Elder
        Sambucus pubens Michx. 18[1]

23. Buds sticky; nearly black. Horsechestnut *Aesculus hippo-*
    castanum L.
23. Buds not sticky; brownish. Buckeye *Aesculus* spp. 19

[1]Stipule scars sometimes present.

24. Bud scale single, or appearing so - - - - - - - - - - - - - 25
24. Bud scales distinctly two or more; valvate or
    imbricate - 26

25. Buds long, narrow, flattened near the tip; twigs slender.
    Willow; usually Purple Willow *Salix purpurea* L. See also
    No. 108 for illustration.
25. Buds short and plump; twigs moderately stout. Cranberry-
    bush *Viburnum trilobum* Marsh 20

26. Outer scales of terminal bud 2, valvate[1] - - - - - - - - - 27
26. Bud scales more than 2, distinctly imbricate - - - - - - 36

27. Twigs of the season grey, or dull grayish-brown; never
    hairy - 28
27. Twigs of the season often highly colored (red, or reddish-
    brown, green, purple, etc.) - - - - - - - - - - - - - - - - - - - 30

28. Leaf buds narrowly lance shaped; lead colored.
    Nannyberry *Viburnum lentago* L.[2] 21
28. Leaf buds shorter - 29

29. Buds very dark red to dark rusty brown, and scurfy or
    tomentose:
    A. Buds scurfy — Blackhaw *Viburnum prunifolium* L. 22
    AA. Buds tomentose — Rusty Nannyberry *V. rufidulum* Raf. 23
29. Buds lighter in color, not scurfy; twigs usually orange brown,
    brown, grey on older growth. Panicled Dogwood *Cornus
    racemosa* Lam. 30

30. Leaf scars not raised; broadly V-shaped, nearly
    meeting - 31
30. Leaf scars somewhat raised upon the persistent leaf
    bases; U-shaped and connected on each side by a
    narrow line - 32

31. Twigs downy, especially near the tip, buds acute.
    Mountain Maple *Acer spicatum* Lam. 25
31. Twigs glabrous, buds larger, and blunt. Striped Maple
    or Moosewood *Acer pensylvanicum* L. 24

[1]If the terminal bud is poorly developed, the twigs stout, terete, with a
fairly large pith, see No. 37.

[2]Also wildraisin, witherod, *V. cassinoides* L. if rusty, and pitted on the
surface.

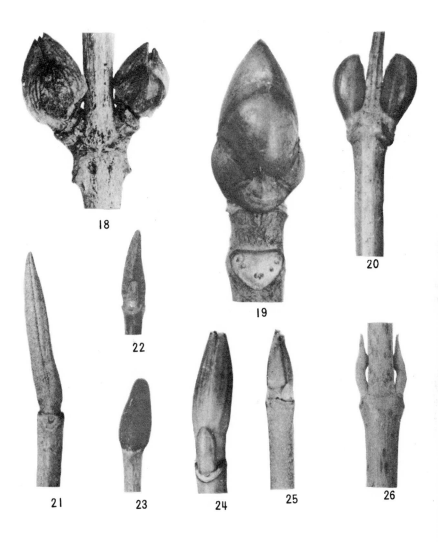

18

19

20

22

21   23   24   25   26

32. Twigs with many conspicuous purple lenticels —
    Roundleaf dogwood *Cornus rugosa* Lam. 26
32. Lenticels not conspicuous, few in number - - - - - - - - 33

33. Twigs bright or dark red - 34
33. Twigs purplish, often angled or diamond shaped in
    cross section; — *or* orange-brown - - - - - - - - - - - - - - - - 35

34. Twigs more or less densely pubescent on the growth of the season; pith brownish. Silky Dogwood *Cornus amomum* Mill.

34. Twigs glabrous; pith white. Redstemmed Dogwood *Cornus stolonifera* Michx. **27**

35. Twigs purplish or bluish, often with a whitish bloom; angled or diamond-shaped. Flowering Dogwood *Cornus florida* L. **28 & 29**

35. Twigs orange-brown, turning to gray the second season; persistent red panicles often present; fruit white. Panicled Dogwood *Cornus racemosa* Lam. **30**

36. Buds blue to reddish-purple and covered with dense white pubescence[1] *or* purplish brown and smooth, (but scales may be ciliate) sap of freshly cut twig milky - **37**

36. Buds orange to bright red; or brown to black, sap clear **38**

37. Buds whitish pubescent; twigs often glaucous; sap clear. Boxelder *Acer negundo* L. **31**

37. Buds smooth, the terminal conspicuous, purplish brown, sap milky. Norway Maple *Acer platanoides* L. **32**

38. Twigs red or orange: when crushed, with a rank odor: Silver Maple *Acer saccharinum* L. **34** Twigs not rank: Red Maple *Acer rubrum* L. Flower buds in both species globose, clustered and conspicuous. **33**

38. Twigs brown to gray - **39**

39. Twigs usually ending in a thorn; buds usually sub-opposite. European Buckthorn *Rhamnus cathartica* L. **35**

39. Twigs never thorny; buds always opposite - - - - - - - - - - - **40**

40. Twigs smooth and shiny with somewhat prominent lenticels. Lenticels large and warty: Black Maple *Acer nigrum* Michx. f. **36**; Lenticels less prominent: Sugar Maple *Acer saccharum* Marsh **37**

40. Twigs dull, sometimes pubescent, lenticels not prominent - **41**

---

[1]Boxelder, which should run out here, is very variable in color and amount of pubescence. If in doubt, compare with Fig. 31.

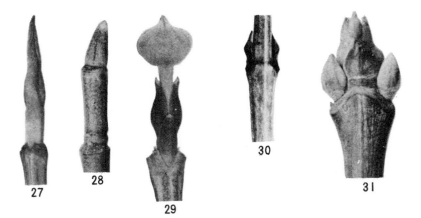

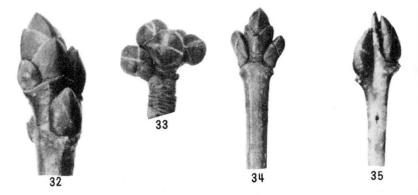

41. Leaf scars small and inconspicuous; considerably raised
    upon persistent leaf bases; buds blunt to acute, with from
    2 to many scales; some species vine-like. Honeysuckle
    Lonicera spp. 38
41. Leaf scars larger, not greatly raised - - - - - - - - - - - - - - 42

    42. Buds with two to three pairs of visible scales - - - - - - 43
    42. Buds with about five pairs of visible scales; terminal
        fruit capsules often persistent. Bush-honeysuckle
        Diervilla lonicera Mill. 39

43. Buds acute, scales apiculate; twigs moderately stout to
    slender - 44
43. Buds obtuse to acute; scales acute; twigs stout; pith large.
    Hydrangea *Hydrangea* spp. 40

44. Twigs usually pubescent, lower scales short. Maple-
leaf Viburnum *Viburnum acerifolium* L. 41
44. Twigs glabrous or nearly so, lower bud scales nearly
half as long as the bud. Arrowwood *Viburnum
dentatum* L. 42

45. Twigs armed with thorns, spines, or stiff bristles - - - - - - 46
45. Twigs unarmed - 62

46. Pith lacking; stem solid; except for scattered pores.
Greenbrier *Smilax* spp. 43
46. Pith present - 47

47. Plants consisting of long, more or less straight, biennial
canes, erect or prostrate; the place of leaf attachment
marked by an irregular stub - 48
47. Perennials, and not as above - - - - - - - - - - - - - - - - - - 51

48. Stems prostrate, usually prickly or bristly. Dewberries
Rubus spp.
48. Stem erect - 49

49. Stems green to greenish red; usually angled in cross
section, armed with large, sharp spines. Blackberries
Rubus spp. 44
49. Stems bluish-white, or purple; circular in cross section - - - 50

50. Stems bluish-white; glaucous; armed with few sharp
spines. Black Raspberries *Rubus* spp. 45
50. Stems purple; clothed with many stiff bristles. Red
Raspberries *Rubus* spp. 46

51. Spines paired at the nodes - 52
51. Spines or thorns solitary, or distributed over the surface
of the stem - 53

52. Buds apparently lacking but submerged beneath the
leaf scar which often shows three irregular cracks.
Robinia spp. : Black Locust *Robinia pseudoacacia* L. 47
52. Buds clearly visible, reddish and wooly. Common
Prickly-ash *Zanthoxylum americanum* Mill. 48

36

37

38

39

40

41

42

43

44

45

46

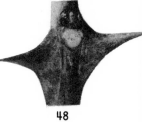

47

48

53. Spines distributed over the surface of the twig - - - - - - - - - 54
53. Spines or thorns solitary at the nodes: or pseudo-terminal
    (branched or unbranched) - 57

    54. Twigs very stout; leaf scars exceptionally large, and
    reaching half way or more around the twig; bundle
    scars 5 or more. Devil's Walkingstick *Aralia spinosa* L. 49
    54. Twigs moderately stout to slender; bundle scars 3,
    sometimes indistinct - 55

55. Twigs ridged or lined from the nodes; bud scales about 6,
    rather loosely covering the bud; epidermis of twig often
    shreddy. Gooseberry *Ribes* spp. 50, 51, 52
55. Twigs not ridged; bud scales 3 or 4, or indistinct; epidermis
    not shreddy - 56

    56. Leaf scars very narrow (line-like) Rose *Rosa* spp. 54
    56. Leaf scars rounded triangular to nearly circular.
    Hercules-club *Zanthoxylum clavaherculis* L. 53

57. Spines slender, single or branched. Barberry *Berberis* spp.[1] 59
57. Thorns or spines moderately stout, single or branched - - - - 58

    58. Thorns 3-branched, or often 2-branched; on old trunks
    commonly many branched; buds nearly hidden beneath
    the leaf scar, but often appearing as small knobs.
    Honeylocust *Gleditsia triacanthos* L. 56 - 57
    58. Thorns or spines single (rarely severally branched on
    old trunks) buds plainly visible, not partially
    submerged - 59

59. Buds acute. Pear *Pyrus communis* L. 55
    (Also certain species of wild apple.)
59. Buds obtuse, or globose - 60

    60. Terminal bud present; bud scales dark red, glabrous,
    somewhat fleshy. Hawthorn *Crataegus* spp. 58
    60. Terminal bud lacking; bud scales not fleshy; brown,
    or rusty tomentose - 61

[1]Also slow growth gooseberry; No. 55.

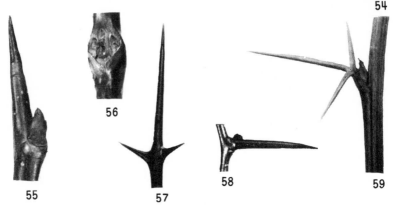

61. Bud scales rusty tomentose. Gum Bumelia *Bumelia lanuginosa* (Michx.) ᐯers. 61
61. Bud scales brown; sap milky. Osage-orange *Maclura pomifera* (Raf.) Schn. 60

    62. Pith chambered[1] - 63
    62. Pith solid, or rarely spongy; in some species small and not readily distinguishable - - - - - - - - - - - - - - - - - - 69

63. Leaf scars broad and conspicuous; shield-shaped, or 3-lobed; bundle scars large and in three groups, usually appearing as 3 small horseshoes - 64
63. Leaf scars half round to narrow or U-shaped; bundle scars appearing as 3 small dots, a straight line, or a crescent - - - 65

---

[1]If vine-like, with mucronate bud scales, and chambered or hollow pith, see No. 71.

64. Pith chocolate brown; leaf scar surmounted by a velvety
    ridge. Butternut *Juglans cinerea* L. 62
64. Pith buff colored; upper edge of leaf scar smooth.
    Black Walnut *Juglans nigra* L. 63
    (62 and 63 reproduced at 1¼×)

65. Stipule scars present; twigs slender, zig-zag; buds closely
    appressed; pith small and often chambered only at the nodes,
    solid elsewhere. Hackberry *Celtis* spp. 64
65. Stipule scars lacking; twigs nearly straight; buds not
    appressed; pith usually completely chambered except for
    short intervals between the season's growth - - - - - - - - - - 66

66. Bundle scars 3, twigs green. Sweetspire *Itea virginica* L.
66. Bundle scar appearing as a straight line or crescent;
    occasionally seen to consist of numerous small scars
    placed closely together - - - - - - - - - - - - - - - - - - - 67

67. Bud scales 2, greatly overlapping; twigs often velvety.
    Persimmon *Diospyros virginiana* L. 65
67. Bud scales about 4 in number - - - - - - - - - - - - - - - - - - 68

68. Buds ovoid, acute; bark on older twigs shreddy.
    Silverbell *Halesia carolina* L. 66
68. Buds conical, obtuse; bark not shreddy; leaves often
    persistent, especially in the southern part of its range.
    Sweetleaf *Symplocos tinctoria* (L.) L'Her. 67

69. Woody vines - 70
69. Shrubby or arborescent - 74

70. Leaf scars narrow, U- or V-shaped; bundle scars 3;
    buds superposed upon a hairy patch between the sides
    of the leaf scar. Dutchman's Pipe *Aristolochia* spp. 68
70. Leaf scars half round to broadly oval; bundle scars
    single; *or* scars several in an often inconspicuous oval,
    ellipse, or C-shaped line - - - - - - - - - - - - - - - - - - 71

71. Bundle scar single, bud scales with mucronate tips.
    Waxwork or Bittersweet *Celastrus scandens* L. 69
71. Bundle scars several; bud scales not mucronate - - - - - - - 72

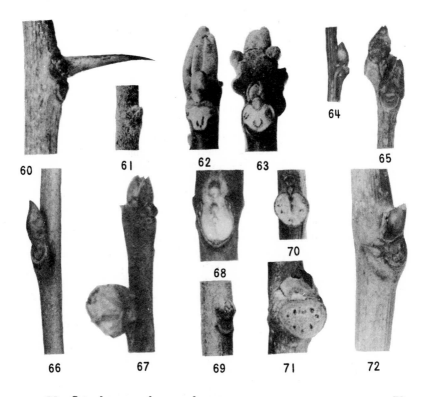

72. Stipule scars long and narrow - - - - - - - - - - - - - - - - - 73
72. Stipule scars lacking; stems fluted; leaf scars somewhat
    raised; bundle scars often in a saucer-like depression.
    Moonseed *Menispermum canadense* L. 70

73. Pith homogeneous except for a bar of darker tissue at each
    node. Grape *Vitis* spp. 72
73. Pith often somewhat spongy, sometimes chambered at the
    edges, not separated by darker bars at the nodes. Woodbine
    or Virginia Creeper *Parthenocissus* spp. 71

74. Pith diaphragmed[1] - 75
74. Pith homogeneous, rarely spongy; (sometimes small
    and not readily distinguishable - - - - - - - - - - - - - - - 78

[1]This does not include those twigs which have a band of firmer tissue
at each node only.

75. Stipule scars appearing as a line encircling the twig, bundle
    scars numerous - 76
75. Stipule scars lacking; bundle scars conspicuous, 3 to 5 in
    in number - 77

  76. Terminal buds with 2 outer scales; flattened, glabrous;
      leaf scars nearly circular; bundle scars numerous,
      scattered in an irregular ellipse. Yellow-poplar or
      Tuliptree *Liriodendron tulipifera* L. 73
  76. Terminal buds single scaled; not flattened; leaf scars
      U-shaped to circular; bundle scars numerous and more
      or less scattered. Magnolia *Magnolia* spp. such as
      Cucumbertree *M. acuminata* L. 74

77. Buds naked, dark red; bundle scars 5 to 7. Pawpaw *Asimina*
    triloba (L.) Dunal. See No. 97
77. Buds scaly; bundle scars 3. Tupelo *Nyssa* spp. such as Black
    Tupelo *N. sylvatica* Marsh. 75 and Water Tupelo *N. aquatica* L.76

  78. Twigs bearing minute yellow globose resin droplets
      visible only with a hand lens - - - - - - - - - - - - - - - - 79
  78. Resin droplets lacking (do not mistake lenticels for
      these) - 80

79. Stipule scars present. Sweetfern *Comptonia peregrina* (L.)
    Coult. (If not aromatic, see Gray Birch, p. 44)
79. Stipule scars lacking. Bayberry *Myrica* spp. 77 (If strongly
    decurrent at the nodes, see also *Ribes* No. 134)

  80. Leaf scars minute, numerous, in evident spirals; bundle
      scars single; twigs lined from the leaf scars; buds less
      in number than the leaf scars; spur shoots conspicuous
      on older growth. Larch *Larix* spp. Tamarack *L. laricina*
      (DuRoi) K. Koch 78-79
  80. Twigs not as above - 81

81. Buds apparently lacking[1]; almost or entirely hidden by the
    leaf scar or submerged beneath it, superposed buds sometimes
    barely visible with a lens - 82
81. Buds (terminals, laterals, or both) present - - - - - - - - - - - 84

_____

[1]Cylindrical, many-scaled catkins should not be mistaken for buds.

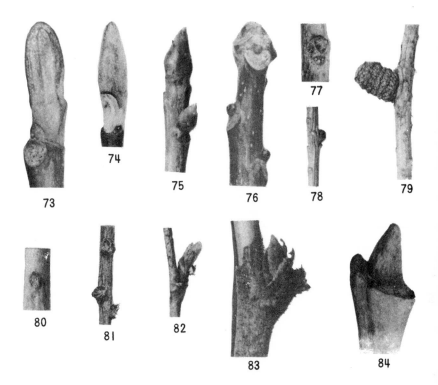

82. Twigs with a strong aromatic odor when crushed; buds
    covered with yellow hair, and only visible after the leaf
    scar bearing portion of the twig is carefully removed;
    sap milky. Fragrant Sumac *Rhus aromatica* Ait. 80
82. Twigs not aromatic; buds almost or entirely submerged
    beneath the leaf scar; sap clear - - - - - - - - - - - - - - - 83

83. Buds completely submerged; twigs usually with stipular
    spines. Locust *Robinia* spp. See also No. 52
83. Buds nearly submerged but often appearing as small rounded
    outgrowths; twigs usually armed with branched thorns.
    Honeylocust *Gleditsia* spp. See also No. 58

84. Leaf scars lacking, or if present raised upon short stubs
    (Fig. 83) or long persistent leaf bases, often slender,
    clasping and not readily recognized - - - - - - - - - - - - 85
84. Leaf scars present (use hand lens if necessary) never
    more than moderately raised, or level with the twig - - - 87

85. Leaf scars lacking[1]; buds very small, rounded and appearing partly submerged in the twig; small round pits usually
present on the surface. Baldcypress *Taxodium distichum* (L.)
Rich 81

85. Leaf scars inconspicuous, and raised upon short stubs or
long slender often clasping leaf bases - - - - - - - - - - - - - - 86

  86. Leaf base very long and slender, clasping; bearing
  persistent stipules; low shrubby perennials. Cinquefoil
  Potentilla fruticosa L. 82

  86. Leaf base shorter, moderately stout, stipules sometimes
  present; tall biennial canes. Flowering Raspberry *Rubus*
  spp. 83

87. Stipule scars continuous, forming a closed ring about the
twig (See Plate I, Fig. 6) - 88

87. Stipule scars lacking, or if present not continuous - - - - - - - 89

  88. Terminal bud lacking; twigs zig-zag; buds resinous
  within, and covered with a single, glabrous, cap-like
  scale; leaf scars nearly encircling the buds. American
  Sycamore or Planetree *Platanus occidentalis* L. 84

  88. Terminal bud present, usually large and conspicuous;
  twigs nearly straight; bud scale pubescent in most
  species; leaf scars U-shaped or broad. Magnolia *Magnolia* spp. See also No. 76

89. Freshly cut twigs with a spicy (sassafras), or wintergreen
taste or odor - 90

89. Twigs lacking a spicy or wintergreen taste or odor - - - - - - 93

  90. Twigs with a wintergreen taste - - - - - - - - - - - - - - - - 91
  90. Twigs spicy - 92

91. Buds sharp to the touch, the laterals divergent, mostly
glabrous; twigs brown and very aromatic. Sweet Birch
Betula lenta L. 85 spur shoot; 86 false terminal.

91. Buds not as sharp, often appressed along the lower half,
often hairy; twigs greenish brown, less aromatic. Yellow
Birch *Betula alleghaniensis* Britton (*B. lutea* Michx. f.)
(Twigs of these two species are often difficult to separate from each other.)

[1]What may appear to be leaf scars are lacking in bundle scars.

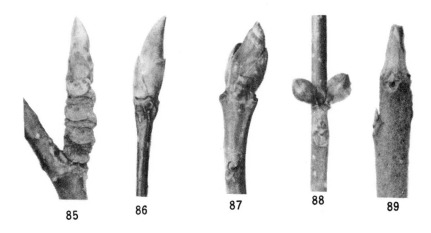

85   86   87   88   89

92. Buds usually solitary; twigs bright green. Sassafras
   Sassafras albidum (Nutt.) Nees. **87**
92. Buds commonly collateral and superposed; flower buds
   nearly spherical; twigs olive-brown. Spicebush *Lindera
   benzoin* (L.) Bl. **88**

93. Buds naked (See Plate I, Fig. 4), or only indistinctly scaly
   on account of a covering of hair or wool; in some species
   small and partly submerged - **94**
93. Buds scaly with one or more scales; glabrous or pubescent -**108**

94. Terminal bud present, larger than the laterals - - - - - - - **95**
94. Terminal bud lacking, or if present not larger than
   the laterals[1] - **100**

95. Bundle scar single, large and protruding; buds silvery
   pubescent. Cinnamon Clethra *Clethra acuminata* Michx. **89**
95. Bundle scar appearing as a curved line, or scars 3 or more - **96**

96. Buds wholly or partially covered with gray, or very
   dark red wool or hair - **97**
96. Buds greenish yellow, tan colored, or brown to black - - **98**

[1]In Witch-hazel, the presence of large, superposed buds may be con-
fusing. If in doubt, compare with Fig. 92.

97. Buds very dark red, hairy; leaf buds long and narrow,
flower buds somewhat globose. Pawpaw *Asimina triloba* (L.)
Dunal 90-91

97. Buds more or less grayish wooly; leaf and flower buds
similar; terminal bud ovoid to globose; twigs with a characteristic semi-sweet taste. Apple *Malus* spp. See also No.129

    98. Stipule scars lacking; leaf scars large and shield-
    shaped, or lobed; bundle scars conspicuous, grouped;
    pith 5-angled. Pecan Hickories *Carya* spp. See key to
    species page 43.

    98. Stipule scars or stipules present; leaf scars small and
    not lobed - 99

99. Buds greenish yellow or tan colored, sometimes with a
pair of small inconspicuous scales near the base; stipules
deciduous. Witch-hazel *Hamamelis virginiana* L. 92

99. Buds brownish, entirely naked; stipules persistent or
deciduous. Carolina Buckthorn *Rhamnus caroliniana* Walt.

    100. Twigs with a peculiar jointed appearance; bark of
    twigs very tough; buds widely conical, silky, partially
    covered by the membranous leaf scar. Leatherwood
    Dirca palustris L. 93

    100. Twigs not as above - 101

101. Leaf scars broad and shield shaped; buds small and
partly sunken in a hairy crater; twigs very stout; pith
reddish. Kentucky coffeetree *Gymnocladus dioicus* (L.)
K. Koch. 94

101. Leaf scars small, or narrow and often nearly encircling
the buds; pith white, green or yellowish - - - - - - - - - - - - 102

    102. Bundle scars single, often partially torn and
    indistinct - 103

    102. Bundle scars 3 or more - - - - - - - - - - - - - - - - - - - 104

103. Buds superposed. Storax *Styrax* spp. 95

103. Buds solitary or collateral. Hardhack, or Steeplebush
Spiraea tomentosa L. 96

    104. Sap from a freshly cut twig milky - - - - - - - - - - - - - 105

    104. Sap not milky - 107

105. Twigs glabrous. Smooth Sumac *Rhus glabra* L.

105. Twigs conspicuously hairy or covered with a fine wool - - 106

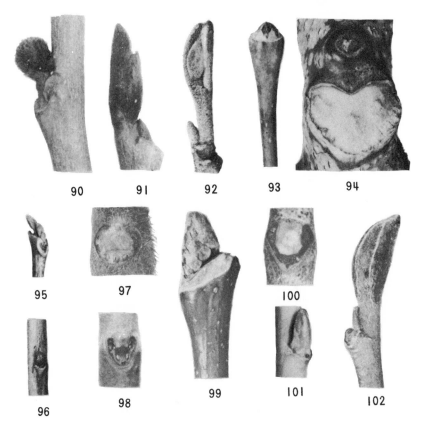

90   91   92   93   94

95   97   100

96   98   99   101   102

106. Twigs hairy; pith yellowish and very large.
     Staghorn Sumac *Rhus typhina* L. 97
106. Twigs covered with a fine wool; pith greenish white.
     Shining Sumac *Rhus copallina* L. 98

107. Buds ovoid, brownish,[1] composed of several closely packed
     units; leaf scars nearly encircling the bud. Yellowwood
     Cladrastis lutea (Michx. f.) K. Koch. 99
107. Buds depressed conical, silvery silky; leaf scars horse-
     shoe-shaped. Hoptree or wafer-ash *Ptelea trifoliata* L. 100

     108. Bud scale single, forming a cap-like covering for
          the bud; buds commonly flattened; twigs usually
          slender. Willow *Salix* spp. 101
     108. Bud scales 2 or more -109

[1]Buds red may be spineless prickly-ash (see No. 52).

109. Buds distinctly stalked; pith triangular in cross section;
      usually visible without a lens. Alder *Alnus* spp. Speckled
      Alder *A. rugosa* (DuRoi) Spreng.[1] 102
109. Without the above combination of characters - - - - - - - - - 110

   110. Bundle scar single (one); appearing as a dot,
       straight line, or curve - 111
   110. Bundle scars 2 or more - - - - - - - - - - - - - - - - - - - 119

111. Buds small, globose, covered by several mucronate
      tipped scales; usually twining shrubs or vine-like.
      Waxwork or Bittersweet *Celastrus scandens* L. See also No. 71
111. Bud scales not mucronate; shrubby or arborescent - - - - - 112

   112. Stipules small, persistent or deciduous - - - - - - - - - 113
   112. Stipules or stipule scars lacking - - - - - - - - - - - - - 115

113. A low, scarcely hardy shrub; fruit a dry capsule, the
      disk-like base commonly persistent on the twig.
      Jerseytea *Ceanothus americanus* L. 103 - 104
113. Usually tall shrubs, or arborescent; fruit fleshy,
      sometimes persistent during the winter - - - - - - - - - - - - 114

   114. Stipules often persistent as minute spines; buds
       nearly globose, bundle scars always single. Holly
       Ilex spp. 105
   114. Without the above combination of characters; bundle
       scars sometimes indistinctly 3 in number. Buckthorn
       Rhamnus spp. 106

115. Bud scales minutely ciliate on the margin, otherwise
      glabrous; twigs purplish. Mountainholly *Nemopanthus*
      mucronata (L.) Trel. 107 - 108
115. Bud scales not ciliate, or if so also more or less hairy
      over their entire surface; twigs not purplish - - - - - - - - - 116

   116. Terminal bud lacking; bud scales 2, greatly over-
       lapping; pith often chambered. Persimmon *Diospyros*
       virginiana L. See No. 67.
   116. Terminal bud present or lacking; bud scales 2 or more,
       not greatly overlapping; pith never chambered - - - - 117

---

[1]*A. serrulata*, the more southern species formerly called *A. rugosa*, has
smaller, more ovoid buds.

    A. crispa, an Arctic species found in mountainous regions of some of
the northern states, does not have stalked buds.

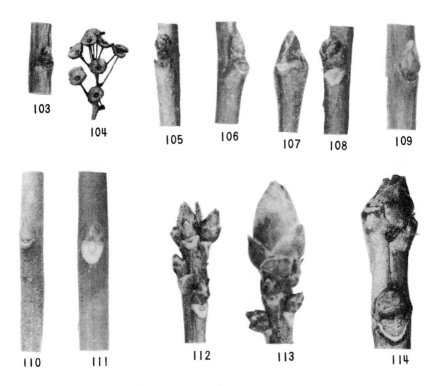

117. Bundle scar very large and protruding; leaf scar triangular, indented on the upper edge. Pepperbush *Clethra alnifolia* L.

117. Bundle scar smaller and not protruding; leaf scars usually not triangular but if so, not indented - - - - - - - - - - - - - - 118

    118. Leaf scars uneven or rough; bark tending to peel; stems often wand-like, much branched with slender tips. Spirea *Spiraea* spp. 109

    118. Without the above combination of characters. The Heath Plants Ericaceae[1] such as Blueberry *Vaccinium* spp. 110; Sourwood *Oxydendrum arboreum* (L.) De Cand. 111; and Azalea *Rhododendron* spp. 112-113

[1]Many of the deciduous heath plants are difficult to separate in winter. The heath family is an interesting one, in that its various representatives are usually associated with a bog habitat or similar situation where the soil is acid in character.

119. Bundle scars 2, stout spur shoots present on older growth;
bark fibrous and shreddy. Ginkgo (*Ginkgo biloba* L.) 114
119. Bundle scars 3 or more, and without the remaining combination of characters - 120

    120. Length of terminal bud more than four times its
    diameter at the base - - - - - - - - - - - - - - - - - - - 121
    120. Terminal bud lacking or if present, not as above,
    usually ovoid to globose - - - - - - - - - - - - - - - - 125

121. First (lowermost) scale of the lateral bud directly over the
leaf scar (See Fig. 115). Poplars: key to species on page 42.
121. First scale of the lateral bud partly to one side of the
leaf scar; or not readily distinguishable - - - - - - - - - - - - 122

    122. Stipule scars long and narrow, nearly encircling
    the twig; buds lance-shaped with about 8 or more
    visible scales; twigs tough, at first brown, later
    gray. American Beech *Fagus grandifolia* Ehr. 116
    122. Stipule scars lacking; buds with not more than 6
    visible scales - 123

123. Bundle scars 3; twigs with a bitter almond taste - - - - - - 124
123. Bundle scars about 10; tissue lemon yellow when sec-
tioned. Yellowroot *Xanthoriza simplicissima* Marsh. 117

    124. Second bud scale one half or more the length of the
    bud. Chokeberry *Pyrus melanocarpa* (Michx.) Willd. 118
    124. Second bud scale less than half the length of the
    bud. Serviceberry or Shadbush *Amelanchier* spp.;
    a common species is *A. arborea* Fern. (formerly
    A. canadensis Med.)

125. Pith 4- to 5-angled or star shaped in cross-section [1] - - - 126
125. Pith circular or nearly so[2]; or in some species very
small and nearly triangular - - - - - - - - - - - - - - - - - - - 133

---

[1] Several smooth sections should be made across the twig between
nodes to see this feature.

[2] If the bundle scars are ring-like with dark centers, see No. 131.

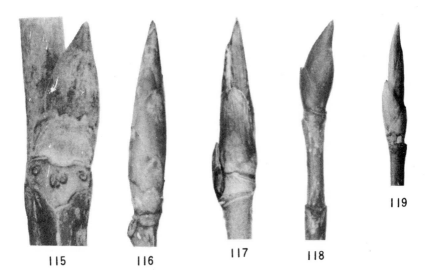

115   116   117   118   119

126. First scale of the lateral bud large and directly
     above the leaf scar. (Fig. 115). Aspens and other
     Poplars: key to species on page 42.
126. First scale of the lateral bud partly to one side
     of the leaf scar (not directly above it); or small
     and not readily distinguishable - - - - - - - - - - - - - 127

127. Bud scales numerous and arranged in 5 more or less
     distinct rows or ranks; buds usually clustered at the
     ends of the twigs; terminal bud about the same size
     as the clustered laterals. Oaks *Quercus*. See key to
     species on page 45.
127. Bud scales from 2 to about 6 in number; not 5-ranked;
     buds rarely clustered - 128

   128. Leaf scars usually lobed, frequently large and
        shield shaped; bundle scars numerous; terminal
        bud present. Hickories *Carya* spp. Key to species
        on page 43.
   128. Leaf scars half round, or narrow and curved;
        bundle scars 3 or in 3 groups - - - - - - - - - - - - - 129

129. Leaf scars narrow, slightly curved, twigs with a characteristic semi-sweet taste; buds often whitish wooly. Apple *Malus pumila* Mill. 120; Buds glabrous or brownish hairy. Pear *Pyrus communis* L. 121
129. Leaf scars half round to elliptical - - - - - - - - - - - - - - - - 130

    130. Twigs with a rank disagreeable bitter-almond taste. Cherry, Peach and Plum *Prunus* spp. Mazzard Cherry *P. avium* (L.) L. 122; Choke cherry *P. virginiana* L., with grey margined scales 123; Black cherry *P. serotina* Ehrh. 124; Fire cherry *P. pensylvanica* L. f., buds small, rounded and clustered 125
    130. Twigs lacking a bitter taste - - - - - - - - - - - - - - - - 131

131. Bundle scars ring-like with dark centers; twigs greenish; older twigs often corky. Sweetgum *Liquidambar styraciflua* L. 126
131. Bundle scars not ring-like; twigs chestnut brown, or grayish, never corky - 132

    132. Twigs and buds chestnut brown, glabrous. American Chestnut[1] *Castanea dentata* (Marsh) Bork. 127
    132. Twigs and buds grayish wooly. Allegheny Chinkapin *Castanea pumila* (L.) Mill. 128

133. Twigs ridged or lined from the nodes; epidermis soon cracking or shredding; bud scales somewhat loose - - - - - 134
133. Twigs usually not ridged; epidermis not shreddy - - - - - - 135

    134. Stipule scars present; bundle scars 5, very unequal in size. Ninebark *Physocarpus opulifolius* (L.) Maxim. 129
    134. Stipule scars lacking; bundle scars 3. Currant or Spineless Gooseberry *Ribes* spp. 130

135. Low, often scarcely hardy shrubs - - - - - - - - - - - - - - - - 136
135. Hardy shrubs, or arborescent - - - - - - - - - - - - - - - - - - 137

    136. Leaf scars long and very narrow. Rose *Rosa* spp. See also No. 56
    136. Leaf scars half round; the disk-like persistent fruit bases often present. Jerseytea *Ceanothus americanus* L. See also No. 113

---

[1]If buds are sunken, and sometimes superposed, see Honeylocust, No. 58.

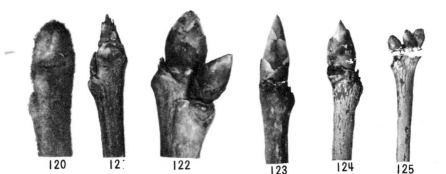

120 12: 122 123 124 125

126 127 128 129 130

137. Terminal bud present - 138
137. Terminal bud lacking - 143

    138. Terminal bud large and conspicuous, scales some-
        what hairy; Rowan-tree, or European Mountainash
        Sorbus aucuparia L. 131; *or* buds essentially glabrous[1];
        American Mountainash *Sorbus americana* Marsh. 132
    138. Terminal bud smaller (compare with Figs. 131 and
        132) - 139

139. Buds and leaf scars small, the edges of the latter show-
    ing minute folds or wrinkles; twigs shiny, when freshly cut
    aromatic with a pleasant fruity odor. Smoketree *Cotinus* spp. 133
139. Leaf scars not wrinkled on the edges, or twigs not aromatic
    as above - 140

[1]Scales may be ciliate.

140. Bud scales reddish, thick, somewhat fleshy; buds
     often gummy when pressed between the fingers.
     Hawthorn *Crataegus* spp. 134. See also No. 60.
140. Buds without the above combination of characters - - 141

141. Visible bud scales usually 2 or 3; twigs green to purple.
     Alternate-leaf or Pagoda Dogwood *Cornus alternifolia* L.f. 135
141. Visible bud scales mostly 4 or more - - - - - - - - - - - - - - - 142

    142. Stipule remnants or scars present; twigs usually with
         a disagreeable bitter-almond taste. Cherry, Plum and
         Peach *Prunus* spp. See also No. 130.
    142. Stipule scars lacking; twigs with a characteristic
         semi-sweet taste. Apple *Malus pumila* Mill., and
         Pear *Pyrus communis* L. See also No. 129.

143. Twigs stout; leaf scars large, conspicuous and shield-
     shaped - 144
143. Twigs slender or moderately so; leaf scars small; half
     round, elliptical, or narrow and inconspicuous - - - - - - - - 145

    144. Buds solitary, bundle scars about 9, arranged along
         or near the edge of the leaf scar. Ailanthus or Tree-
         of-Heaven *Ailanthus altissima* (Mill.) Swing. 136
    144. Buds superposed; bundle scars 3, usually curved,
         not always distinct. Soapberry *Sapindus drummondii*
         Hook and Arn.

145. Stipule scars lacking - 146
145. Stipule scars present - 148

    146. Upper edge of leaf scar unevenly fringed; buds small
         and obtuse; twigs dark brownish red. Eastern Redbud
         or Judas-tree *Cercis canadensis* L. 137
    146. Leaf scar not fringed; buds nearly globose, often
         depressed - 147

147. Buds solitary or collateral; sap more or less milky (twigs
     usually armed). *Bumelia* spp. See also No. 61.
147. Buds often superposed; sap clear (twigs usually armed).
     Honeylocust *Gleditsia triacanthos* L. See also No. 58.

    148. Outer bud scales usually 2 - - - - - - - - - - - - - - - - - 149
    148. Outer bud scales 3 or more - - - - - - - - - - - - - - - - - 150

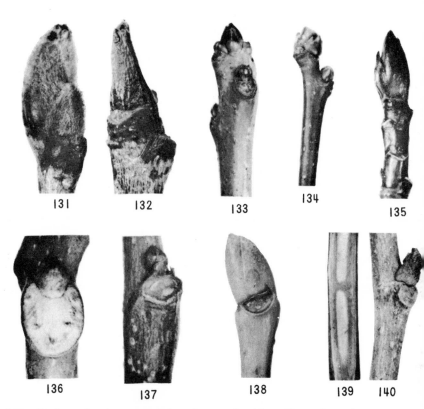

131   132   133   134   135

136   137   138   139   140

149. Buds and twigs greenish red, or red; pith uniform throughout; sap clear. Basswood *Tilia* spp. 138
149. Buds and twigs greenish brown; pith with a transverse par-
tition at each node; sap milky. Paper-mulberry *Broussonetia
papyrifera* (L.) Vent. 139-140

   150. Visible bud scales 3 or 4 (except on spur shoots when
         present); the first pair of scales forming a V-shaped
         angle above the leaf scar; lenticels on older twigs
         elongated horizontally; buds more or less resinous
         when pressed between the fingers; bark on older trees
         papery or scaly. Birches *Betula* spp. See key to species
         on page 44.
   150. Visible bud scales usually more than 4; spur shoots
         lacking; lenticels not elongated horizontally; bark
         never papery - 151

151. Buds closely appressed; twigs conspicuously zig-zag; pith
     intermittently chambered. Hackberry *Celtis* spp. See also No. 65
151. Without the above combination of characters - - - - - - - - - -152

    152. Bundle scars usually numerous; often forming an
         ellipse; sap from a freshly cut twig milky. Mulberry
         Morus spp. ; Red Mulberry *M. rubra* L. 141
    152. Bundle scars 3 or in 3 groups; sap clear - - - - - - - - 153

153. Bundle scars somewhat depressed; leaf scars covered
     with a corky layer - 154
153. Bundle scars not depressed; often slightly raised; leaf
     scars not corky - 157

    154. Older twigs often corky - - - - - - - - - - - - - - - - - 155
    154. Older twigs never corky - - - - - - - - - - - - - - - - - 156

155. Buds very sharply pointed. Rock or Cork Elm *Ulmus
     thomasii* Sarg. 142
155. Buds acute but not sharp. Southern Elms *Ulmus* spp.
     viz. Cedar Elm, Red Elm, and Winged Elm.

    156. Buds dark colored, nearly black; the flower buds
         particularly with orange tips; twigs rough, ashy grey
         in color. Slippery Elm *Ulmus rubra* Mühl. (*U. fulva*
         Michx.) 143
    156. Buds and twigs brown, sometimes pubescent.
         American Elm *Ulmus americana* L. 144

157. Buds of two distinct sizes; both types somewhat angled;
     scales without evident striations or lines; catkins Fig. 148
     lacking; bark of trunk smooth, bluish grey; trunk with a
     twisted or fluted appearance. American Hornbeam *Carpinus
     caroliniana* Walt. 145
157. Buds of uniform size, not angled; catkins often present - - 158

    158. Bud scales marked by fine longitudinal striations;
         use hand lens; bark of trunk finely shaggy. Hop
         Hornbeam *Ostrya virginiana* (Mill.) K. Koch. 146
    158. Bud scales not striated; bark not shaggy, shrubby - - 159

159. Outer bud scales persistent. Hazelnut *Corylus americana* Walt.
159. Outer scales soon deciduous. Beaked Hazelnut *Corylus
     cornuta* Marsh. 147- 148

141   142   143   144

146

147   148

145

ILLUSTRATIONS ON THE FOLLOWING
PAGES REPRODUCED AT 1½×.

Key to Aspens, Cottonwoods, and other Poplars

1. Lateral buds with more than 4 exposed
   scales; buds essentially non-resinous - - - - 2
1. Lateral buds mostly with 3 or 4 visible
   scales; buds resinous when squeezed[1] - - - 3

I   2

   2. Twigs and buds somewhat shiny or
      varnished; the latter brown to nearly
      black; often appressed. Quaking Aspen
      Populus tremuloides Michx. 1
   2. Twigs and buds greyish, dull; the
      latter usually divergent. Bigtooth
      Aspen *Populus grandidentata* Michx.[2] 2

3. Terminal buds mostly ½" or more in length - 4
3. Terminal buds less than ½" long - - - - - - - 6

3

   4. Buds and twigs brownish red, the former
      very resinous, with a fragrant odor when
      crushed. Balsam Poplar *Populus balsami-*
      fera L. (*P. tacamahaca* Mill.) 3
   4. Buds and twigs straw colored (yellow to
      yellowish brown); buds resinous but not
      excessively - - - - - - - - - - - - - - - - - - 5

5. Buds widest at the base, and tapering towards the apex. Carolina Poplar ×*Populus*
   eugenei Schelle 4
5. Buds widest near the middle, and tapering
   both ways. Eastern Cottonwood *Populus*
   deltoides Bartr. 5

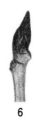

4   5

   6. Buds short and stout. Swamp Cottonwood
      Populus heterophylla L.
   6. Buds more slender and tapering; form of
      tree fastigiate. Lombardy Poplar *Populus*
      nigra var. *italica* Muenchh. 6

6

[1]The buds of quaking aspen may be moderately resinous; therefore use
illustrations for final check.

[2]If the twigs are more or less hairy or tomentose, they are probably from
European White Poplar *P. alba* L. or one of its varieties.

Key to the Common Hickories

1. Bud scales paired, valvate; buds often
   appearing naked - - - - - - - - - - - - - - - - - 2
1. Bud scales imbricate, usually more than
   2 visible - 3

   2. Buds bright yellow. Bitternut Hickory
     Carya cordiformis (Wangenh.) K. Koch. 1
   2. Buds brownish. Pecan Hickory *Carya
     illinoensis* (Wang.) K. Koch. 2

3. Terminal buds short and stout; somewhat
   globose, usually glabrous. Pignut Hickory
   Carya glabra (Mill.) Sweet; and Red Hickory
   Carya ovalis (Wang.) Sarg. 3
   The 1953 "Checklist" considers *C. ovalis*
   a synonym for *C. glabra.*

3. Terminal buds larger, more ellipsoidal, more
   or less hairy - - - - - - - - - - - - - - - - - - - 4

   4. Outer scales soon deciduous, showing
     the lighter colored ones beneath; twigs
     often hairy, and quite fragrant when
     bruised. Mockernut Hickory *Carya to-
     mentosa* Nutt. 4
   4. Outer scales persistent, twigs less
     hairy, or glabrous - - - - - - - - - - - - - - 5

5. Twigs orange-brown, or buff colored, lenticels orange colored. Shellbark Hickory
   Carya laciniosa (Michx. f.) Loud.
5. Twigs dark reddish brown. Shagbark Hickory
   Carya ovata (Mill.) K. Koch. 5

Key to the Birches

1. Twigs with a wintergreen taste - - - - - - - - - - - 2
1. Twigs lacking a wintergreen taste - - - - - - - - - - 3

    2. Buds sharply pointed, divergent, mostly
       glabrous; twigs brown to black, very aro-
       matic. Sweet Birch *Betula lenta* L. See Figs. 85-86.
    2. Buds acute but not sharp to the touch, often
       appressed along the lower half, often hairy;
       twigs greenish brown; less aromatic. Yellow
       Birch *Betula alleghaniensis* Britton (*B. lutea*
       Michx.)

1

3. Buds short, tapering both ways from the middle;
   twigs grayish with very prominent warty lenticels; bark on older branches and trunk grayish
   white, usually close with few exfoliating strips.
   Gray Birch *Betula populifolia* Marsh. 1
3. Buds longer (see Figs. 1 and 2), tapering from
   the base to the apex; twigs brown to nearly
   black, usually with less prominent lenticels;
   bark of tree salmon red, or chalky white, exfoliating in thin papery strips - - - - - - - - - - - - 4

2

    4. Twigs and buds mostly glabrous; the former
       nearly black; bark of tree chalky white. Paper
       Birch *Betula papyrifera* Marsh. 2
    4. Twigs and buds somewhat hairy; the former
       reddish brown; bark of tree salmon red. River
       or Red Birch *Betula nigra* L.

Key to Some Common Eastern Oaks[1]

1. Largest terminal buds mostly ¼" to 3/8"
   long,[2] usually acute - - - - - - - - - - - - - - 2
1. Largest terminals usually less than ¼" to
   3/8" long, acute, obtuse, or globose - - - - -8

   2. Buds distinctly angled in cross-section - 3
   2. Buds circular or only slightly angled
      in cross-section - - - - - - - - - - - - - - - 6

3. Buds usually smooth, rarely downy, dull
   straw colored. Shumard Oak *Quercus shu-
   mardii* Buckl.
3. Buds pubescent, wholly or in part; dark
   red or gray -4

   4. Buds whitish pubescent only toward the
      tip, often obtuse. Scarlet Oak *Quercus
      coccinea* Muenchh. 1
   4. Buds grayish to rusty tomentose; most-
      ly long and acute - - - - - - - - - - - - - - 5

5. Buds grayish wooly; twigs often shiny.
   Black Oak *Quercus velutina* Lam. 2
5. Buds rusty (reddish brown) wooly; twigs
   usually dull, often minutely hairy. Black
   Jack Oak *Quercus marilandica* Muenchh. 3

   6. Buds and twigs orange-brown; buds
      slender and acute; first year acorns
      lacking. Chestnut Oak *Quercus prinus*
      L. (*Q. montana* Willd.) 4
   6. Buds and twigs reddish brown, or the
      former dark red to nearly black, buds
      more plump, obtuse to acute; first
      year acorns present or lacking - - - - - - 7

[1]Northern Pin Oak or Hill's Oak *Q. ellipsoidalis* Hill of the Lake States, has buds similar to those of scarlet oak but smaller (about 1/8'' long).

[2]It is especially important to secure twigs of normally vigorous growth; unusually slow growing branchlets are often difficult to identify.

7. Buds red to reddish brown; the scales near the tip silky (mostly on the margins). Northern red oak *Quercus rubra* L. (*Q. borealis* Michx.) 5

5

7. Buds reddish brown to nearly black, scales near tip with whitish pubescent surfaces; buds wider than in red oak (see Figs. 1 and 5). Scarlet Oak *Quercus coccinea* Muenchh.

    8. Buds mostly acute - - - - - - - - - - - - - 9
    8. Buds obtuse to nearly globose - - - - - - 12

9. Twigs more or less woolly. Bear or Scrub Oak *Quercus ilicifolia* Wangenh. 6
9. Twigs glabrous - - - - - - - - - - - - - - - - - 10

6

    10. Buds and twigs brown to orange-brown. Chinkapin Oak *Quercus muehlenbergii* Engelm. 7
    10. Buds and twigs red to reddish brown - 11

11. Bud scales glabrous; leaves lobed. Pin Oak *Quercus palustris* Muenchh. 8
11. Bud scales pubescent; leaves not lobed. Shingle Oak *Quercus imbricaria* Michx.

7

    12. Twigs shiny and somewhat purplish, or reddish brown - - - - - - - - - - - - - - 13
    12. Twigs dull, yellowish brown - - - - - - 14

13. Buds globose or nearly so, bud scales glabrous; twigs purplish; first year acorns lacking. White Oak *Quercus alba* L. 9
13. Buds obtuse to acute, often angled, whitish pubescent toward the tip; twigs reddish brown; first year acorns lacking. Scarlet Oak *Quercus coccinea* Muenchh. 10

8

9   10

14. Buds and twigs glabrous; bark on older stems ragged. Swamp White Oak *Quercus bicolor* Willd. 11

14. Buds pubescent or tomentose; twigs more or less tomentose - - - - - - - - - 15

11   12

15. Buds usually not more than 1/16" long; twigs slender. Bear or Scrub Oak *Quercus ilicifolia* Wangenh. 12

15. Buds about 1/8" long; twigs moderately stout - 16

16. Buds reddish brown, globose to ovoid. Post Oak *Quercus stellata* Wangenh. 13

16. Buds gray to yellowish brown, obtuse to nearly acute; stipules often persistent; older twigs often corky. Bur Oak *Quercus macrocarpa* Michx. 14

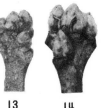

13   14

Key to the Common Ashes

1. Twigs 4-angled, or winged. Blue Ash *Fraxinus quadrangulata* Michx. 1

1. Twigs circular or oval in cross-section - - 2

2. First season's twigs more or less velvety. Green Ash[1] *F. pennsylvanica* Marsh. 2

2. Twigs essentially glabrous - - - - - - - 3

1

3. Leaf scars vertically elliptical to oval; terminal buds conical, brown to black; first pair of lateral buds inserted some distance below the terminal. Black Ash *F. nigra* Marsh. 3

3. Leaf scars half round; first pair of laterals occurring at the base of the terminal bud - - - - - - - - - - - - - - - - - - 4

2   3

[1] Formerly called red ash. Red ash is now synonymous with green ash.

4. Leaf scars usually notched at the top; terminal buds obtuse. White Ash *F. americana* L. 4
4. Leaf scars usually straight on the upper edge; terminal buds acute. Green Ash *F. pennsylvanica* Marsh. 5 (formerly a variety of "red ash")

4   5

ACKNOWLEDGEMENTS

The writer is indebted to Dr. H. P. Brown for helpful suggestions in writing the manuscript; and to Dr. E. S. Harrar of Duke University and Prof. W. H. Pfeiffer of Pennsylvania State College for suggested changes in the Third Edition. Acknowledgment is also due many others for furnishing material of winter twigs. These include the Southern Forest Experiment Station, U. S. Forest Service, New Orleans, La.; the Appalachian Forest Experiment Station, U. S. Forest Service, Asheville, N. C.; Prof. F. C. Gates, Kansas State Agricultural College, Manhattan, Kansas; Dr. C. F. Korstian, Duke University, Durham, N. C.; Prof. J. E. Aughanbaugh, Forest Research Institute, Mont Alto, Pa.; Dr. W. C. Coker, University of North Carolina, Chapel Hill, N. C.; Dr. E. H. Fulling, New York Botanical Garden, New York City; Mr. Erdman West, Florida Experiment Station, Gainesville, Fla.; Dr. M. A. Chrysler, Rutgers University, New Brunswick, N. J.; Dept. of Conservation, New Orleans, La.; Mr. J. F. Lewis, Instructor in Biology, Connellsville, Pa.; and Mr. N. F. Rogers, U.S.F.S., Kenton, Mich.; Mr. David Black, U. S. Forest Service.

SELECTED REFERENCES

1. Billings, W. D. A Bud and Twig Key to the Southeastern Arborescent Oaks. Jour. For. 34:475-476, 1936.
2. Blakeslee, A. F. and Jarvis, C. D. New England Trees in Winter. Bull. 69, Storrs Ag. Exp. Station. 1911.
3. Brown, H. P. Trees of Northeastern U. S. Christopher Pub. Co., Boston. 1938.
4. Fernald, M. L. Gray's Manual of Botany. 8th Ed. Amer. Book Co., New York. 1950.
5. Harlow, W. M. Trees of the Eastern and Central United States and Canada. Dover Publications, New York, 1957.
6. _____ Poisonivy and Poisonsumac. Bul. N. Y. S. Coll. Forestry, Syracuse. 1945.

7. Harrington, H. D. The Woody Plants of Iowa in the Winter Condition. Univ. of Iowa Studies, Vol. XVI. No. 1, June 1, 1934.
8. Kelsey, H. P. and Dayton, W. A. Standardized Plant Names. J. H. McFarland, Harrisburg, Pa. 1942.
9. Little, E. L., Jr. Check List of Native and Naturalized Trees of the United States. U. S. Dept. of Agri., Wash., D. C. 1953.
10. Muenscher, W. C. Keys to Woody Plants, 3rd Ed. Ithaca, N. Y.
11. Sargent, C. S. Manual of the Trees of North America. 2nd Ed. 1926.
12. Trelease, William. Winter Botany. Urbana, Ill.
13. Wiegand, K. M. and Foxworthy, F. W. A Key to the Genera of Woody Plants in Winter. Ithaca, N. Y. 1908.
14. Whelden, C. M. Studies in the Genus Fraxinus I. A Preliminary Key to Winter Twigs for the Sections Melioides and Bumelioides, Jour. Arnold Arb. XV; 118-126, 1934.

A Glossary of Technical Terms Used in The Key

acute   With sides forming an angle of less than 90°.

alternate Said of leaf scars occurring one at each node.

annular   Ring-like; said of leaf scars which encircle the bud, or bundle scars which are circular with an opening in the center.

apiculate Ending in an abrupt pointed tip.

appressed Flattened against the twig.

arborescent Tree-like; defined arbitrarily as pertaining to a woody plant at least 20 ft. high at maturity with a single stem and more or less definite crown.

axillary Said of a bud which is borne directly in the axil or upper angle between leaf and twig.

biennial Ordinarily applied to plants which live but two seasons; during the first season only leaves and stems are produced above ground, while the flowers and seeds are borne the second summer. Here used in a special sense in separating the biennial canes of the raspberries and blackberries from the stems of other woody plants. In these species, the canes themselves are biennial from underground perennial stems.

bundle scars Small dots or lines on the surface of the leaf scar marking the point of original departure of the conducting strands into the leaf.

capsule A dry fruit derived from a compound pistil, and opening in one of a number of ways.

chambered Said of pith when divided into small compartments separated by transverse partitions.

ciliate Hairy on the margin.

collateral Said of extra or supernumerary buds which are inserted on either side of a normal axillary bud.

catkin A compact cylindrical flower cluster composed of numerous flowers subtended by small scales.

continuous Said of pith which is solid; not interrupted by cavities.

deciduous Said of leaves or stipules which do not persist in a green condition throughout the winter; usually falling in the autumn.

diaphragmed Said of pith which is solid with transverse bars of denser tissue at short intervals.

epidermis Outer skin of the twig; sometimes peeling or cracking during the first winter; ultimately destroyed by growth in diameter of the twig.

fluted Grooved.

glabrous Smooth.

glaucous Covered with a white or bluish bloom which can usually be rubbed off easily.

imbricate Said of scales which overlap; the opposite of valvate in which the scales meet along a line without overlapping.

lateral Said of buds which appear along the sides of the twig.

leaf scar A patch differing in color and texture from the rest of the twig and representing the point of attachment of the leaf.

lenticels Small areas of loose tissue which appear as dots or warts on the surface of the twig; not always conspicuous.

lined With narrow longitudinal ridges extending downward from the leaf scars.

mucronate Ending in a fine, slender tip.

naked Said of a bud which is not covered by scales; the outer pair of leaves serves the same purpose.

node The more or less swollen portion of the twig which bears the leaf or leaves.

opposite Said of leaf scars which are paired on opposite sides at each node.

obtuse With sides forming an angle of more than 90°.

ovoid Said of a bud which is egg-shaped, with the broadest portion near the base.

perennials Plants with stems which persist for more than 2 years.

petiole Leaf stem.

prickles Slender, sharp outgrowths of the stem tissues beneath the epidermis.

pubescent Hairy.

scurfy Scaly rather than hairy.

shrubby Applied to woody plants which at maturity are less than 20 ft. high, have more than one stem, and no definite crown shape (a purely arbitrary definition); See also "arborescent"

solitary Single, one.

spines Sharp outgrowths of the twig, sometimes but not always paired at the nodes. Similar to "prickle".

spongy Irregularly interrupted by small, sometimes scarcely distinguishable cavities; porous.

spur-shoots Short stubby branches with greatly crowded leaf scars and very slow growth.

stipules Small leaf-like organs occurring in pairs on either side of the leaves; occasionally each one extends half way around the twig, respectively.

stipule-scars Small marks left by the deciduous stipules.

sub-opposite Said of paired leaf scars which are not at exactly the same height on the twig (staggered)

superposed Said of extra buds which appear above the true axillary buds; usually flower buds.

terminal Applied to the end bud beyond which no further growth takes place normally until the following season.

thorns Sharp outgrowths of the twig which represent modified branches; usually bearing leaf scars, or branched.

tomentose With short matted hairs; woolly.

valvate Applied to bud scales which meet along a definite, usually longitudinal line without overlapping; the reverse of imbricate.

whorled Said of leaf scars which occur three at a node.

— NOTES —

INDEX TO COMMON NAMES

INDEX TO SCIENTIFIC NAMES

A CATALOG OF SELECTED
DOVER BOOKS
IN ALL FIELDS OF INTEREST

A CATALOG OF SELECTED DOVER
BOOKS IN ALL FIELDS OF INTEREST

DRAWINGS OF REMBRANDT, edited by Seymour Slive. Updated Lippmann, Hofstede de Groot edition, with definitive scholarly apparatus. All portraits, biblical sketches, landscapes, nudes. Oriental figures, classical studies, together with selection of work by followers. 550 illustrations. Total of 630pp. 9⅛ × 12¼.
21485-0, 21486-9 Pa., Two-vol. set $25.00

GHOST AND HORROR STORIES OF AMBROSE BIERCE, Ambrose Bierce. 24 tales vividly imagined, strangely prophetic, and decades ahead of their time in technical skill: "The Damned Thing," "An Inhabitant of Carcosa," "The Eyes of the Panther," "Moxon's Master," and 20 more. 199pp. 5⅜ × 8½. 20767-6 Pa. $3.95

ETHICAL WRITINGS OF MAIMONIDES, Maimonides. Most significant ethical works of great medieval sage, newly translated for utmost precision, readability. Laws Concerning Character Traits, Eight Chapters, more. 192pp. 5⅜ × 8½.
24522-5 Pa. $4.50

THE EXPLORATION OF THE COLORADO RIVER AND ITS CANYONS, J. W. Powell. Full text of Powell's 1,000-mile expedition down the fabled Colorado in 1869. Superb account of terrain, geology, vegetation, Indians, famine, mutiny, treacherous rapids, mighty canyons, during exploration of last unknown part of continental U.S. 400pp. 5⅜ × 8½. 20094-9 Pa. $6.95

HISTORY OF PHILOSOPHY, Julián Marías. Clearest one-volume history on the market. Every major philosopher and dozens of others, to Existentialism and later. 505pp. 5⅜ × 8½. 21739-6 Pa. $8.50

ALL ABOUT LIGHTNING, Martin A. Uman. Highly readable non-technical survey of nature and causes of lightning, thunderstorms, ball lightning, St. Elmo's Fire, much more. Illustrated. 192pp. 5⅜ × 8½. 25237-X Pa. $5.95

SAILING ALONE AROUND THE WORLD, Captain Joshua Slocum. First man to sail around the world, alone, in small boat. One of great feats of seamanship told in delightful manner. 67 illustrations. 294pp. 5⅜ × 8½. 20326-3 Pa. $4.95

LETTERS AND NOTES ON THE MANNERS, CUSTOMS AND CONDITIONS OF THE NORTH AMERICAN INDIANS, George Catlin. Classic account of life among Plains Indians: ceremonies, hunt, warfare, etc. 312 plates. 572pp. of text. 6⅛ × 9¼. 22118-0, 22119-9 Pa. Two-vol. set $15.90

ALASKA: The Harriman Expedition, 1899, John Burroughs, John Muir, et al. Informative, engrossing accounts of two-month, 9,000-mile expedition. Native peoples, wildlife, forests, geography, salmon industry, glaciers, more. Profusely illustrated. 240 black-and-white line drawings. 124 black-and-white photographs. 3 maps. Index. 576pp. 5⅜ × 8½. 25109-8 Pa. $11.95

THE BOOK OF BEASTS: Being a Translation from a Latin Bestiary of the Twelfth Century, T. H. White. Wonderful catalog real and fanciful beasts: manticore, griffin, phoenix, amphivius, jaculus, many more. White's witty erudite commentary on scientific, historical aspects. Fascinating glimpse of medieval mind. Illustrated. 296pp. 5⅜ × 8¼. (Available in U.S. only) 24609-4 Pa. $5.95

FRANK LLOYD WRIGHT: ARCHITECTURE AND NATURE With 160 Illustrations, Donald Hoffmann. Profusely illustrated study of influence of nature—especially prairie—on Wright's designs for Fallingwater, Robie House, Guggenheim Museum, other masterpieces. 96pp. 9¼ × 10¾. 25098-9 Pa. $7.95

FRANK LLOYD WRIGHT'S FALLINGWATER, Donald Hoffmann. Wright's famous waterfall house: planning and construction of organic idea. History of site, owners, Wright's personal involvement. Photographs of various stages of building. Preface by Edgar Kaufmann, Jr. 100 illustrations. 112pp. 9¼ × 10.
23671-4 Pa. $7.95

YEARS WITH FRANK LLOYD WRIGHT: Apprentice to Genius, Edgar Tafel. Insightful memoir by a former apprentice presents a revealing portrait of Wright the man, the inspired teacher, the greatest American architect. 372 black-and-white illustrations. Preface. Index. vi + 228pp. 8¼ × 11. 24801-1 Pa. $9.95

THE STORY OF KING ARTHUR AND HIS KNIGHTS, Howard Pyle. Enchanting version of King Arthur fable has delighted generations with imaginative narratives of exciting adventures and unforgettable illustrations by the author. 41 illustrations. xviii + 313pp. 6⅛ × 9¼. 21445-1 Pa. $5.95

THE GODS OF THE EGYPTIANS, E. A. Wallis Budge. Thorough coverage of numerous gods of ancient Egypt by foremost Egyptologist. Information on evolution of cults, rites and gods; the cult of Osiris; the Book of the Dead and its rites; the sacred animals and birds; Heaven and Hell; and more. 956pp. 6⅛ × 9¼.
22055-9, 22056-7 Pa., Two-vol. set $21.90

A THEOLOGICO-POLITICAL TREATISE, Benedict Spinoza. Also contains unfinished *Political Treatise*. Great classic on religious liberty, theory of government on common consent. R. Elwes translation. Total of 421pp. 5⅜ × 8½.
20249-6 Pa. $6.95

INCIDENTS OF TRAVEL IN CENTRAL AMERICA, CHIAPAS, AND YUCATAN, John L. Stephens. Almost single-handed discovery of Maya culture; exploration of ruined cities, monuments, temples; customs of Indians. 115 drawings. 892pp. 5⅜ × 8½. 22404-X, 22405-8 Pa., Two-vol. set $15.90

LOS CAPRICHOS, Francisco Goya. 80 plates of wild, grotesque monsters and caricatures. Prado manuscript included. 183pp. 6⅜ × 9⅜. 22384-1 Pa. $4.95

AUTOBIOGRAPHY: The Story of My Experiments with Truth, Mohandas K. Gandhi. Not hagiography, but Gandhi in his own words. Boyhood, legal studies, purification, the growth of the Satyagraha (nonviolent protest) movement. Critical, inspiring work of the man who freed India. 480pp. 5⅜ × 8½. (Available in U.S. only)
24593-4 Pa. $6.95

SIR HARRY HOTSPUR OF HUMBLETHWAITE, Anthony Trollope. Incisive, unconventional psychological study of a conflict between a wealthy baronet, his idealistic daughter, and their scapegrace cousin. The 1870 novel in its first inexpensive edition in years. 250pp. 5⅜ × 8½.   24953-0 Pa. $4.95

LASERS AND HOLOGRAPHY, Winston E. Kock. Sound introduction to burgeoning field, expanded (1981) for second edition. Wave patterns, coherence, lasers, diffraction, zone plates, properties of holograms, recent advances. 84 illustrations. 160pp. 5⅜ × 8¼. (Except in United Kingdom)   24041-X Pa. $3.50

INTRODUCTION TO ARTIFICIAL INTELLIGENCE: SECOND, EN-LARGED EDITION, Philip C. Jackson, Jr. Comprehensive survey of artificial intelligence—the study of how machines (computers) can be made to act intelligently. Includes introductory and advanced material. Extensive notes updating the main text. 132 black-and-white illustrations. 512pp. 5⅜ × 8½.   24864-X Pa. $8.95

HISTORY OF INDIAN AND INDONESIAN ART, Ananda K. Coomaraswamy. Over 400 illustrations illuminate classic study of Indian art from earliest Harappa finds to early 20th century. Provides philosophical, religious and social insights. 304pp. 6⅜ × 9⅜.   25005-9 Pa. $8.95

THE GOLEM, Gustav Meyrink. Most famous supernatural novel in modern European literature, set in Ghetto of Old Prague around 1890. Compelling story of mystical experiences, strange transformations, profound terror. 13 black-and-white illustrations. 224pp. 5⅜ × 8½. (Available in U.S. only)   25025-3 Pa. $5.95

ARMADALE, Wilkie Collins. Third great mystery novel by the author of *The Woman in White* and *The Moonstone*. Original magazine version with 40 illustrations. 597pp. 5⅜ × 8½.   23429-0 Pa. $7.95

PICTORIAL ENCYCLOPEDIA OF HISTORIC ARCHITECTURAL PLANS, DETAILS AND ELEMENTS: With 1,880 Line Drawings of Arches, Domes, Doorways, Facades, Gables, Windows, etc., John Theodore Haneman. Sourcebook of inspiration for architects, designers, others. Bibliography. Captions. 141pp. 9 × 12.   24605-1 Pa. $6.95

BENCHLEY LOST AND FOUND, Robert Benchley. Finest humor from early 30's, about pet peeves, child psychologists, post office and others. Mostly unavailable elsewhere. 73 illustrations by Peter Arno and others. 183pp. 5⅜ × 8½.
                                                                       22410-4 Pa. $3.95

ERTÉ GRAPHICS, Erté. Collection of striking color graphics: *Seasons, Alphabet, Numerals, Aces* and *Precious Stones*. 50 plates, including 4 on covers. 48pp. 9⅜ × 12¼.   23580-7 Pa. $6.95

THE JOURNAL OF HENRY D. THOREAU, edited by Bradford Torrey, F. H. Allen. Complete reprinting of 14 volumes, 1837–61, over two million words; the sourcebooks for *Walden*, etc. Definitive. All original sketches, plus 75 photographs. 1,804pp. 8½ × 12¼.   20312-3, 20313-1 Cloth., Two-vol. set $80.00

CASTLES: THEIR CONSTRUCTION AND HISTORY, Sidney Toy. Traces castle development from ancient roots. Nearly 200 photographs and drawings illustrate moats, keeps, baileys, many other features. Caernarvon, Dover Castles, Hadrian's Wall, Tower of London, dozens more. 256pp. 5⅜ × 8¼.

                                                                       24898-4 Pa. $5.95

AMERICAN CLIPPER SHIPS: 1833–1858, Octavius T. Howe & Frederick C. Matthews. Fully-illustrated, encyclopedic review of 352 clipper ships from the period of America's greatest maritime supremacy. Introduction. 109 halftones. 5 black-and-white line illustrations. Index. Total of 928pp. 5⅜ × 8½.
25115-2, 25116-0 Pa., Two-vol. set $17.90

TOWARDS A NEW ARCHITECTURE, Le Corbusier. Pioneering manifesto by great architect, near legendary founder of "International School." Technical and aesthetic theories, views on industry, economics, relation of form to function, "mass-production spirit," much more. Profusely illustrated. Unabridged translation of 13th French edition. Introduction by Frederick Etchells. 320pp. 6⅛ × 9¼. (Available in U.S. only)
25023-7 Pa. $8.95

THE BOOK OF KELLS, edited by Blanche Cirker. Inexpensive collection of 32 full-color, full-page plates from the greatest illuminated manuscript of the Middle Ages, painstakingly reproduced from rare facsimile edition. Publisher's Note. Captions. 32pp. 9⅜ × 12¼.
24345-1 Pa. $4.95

BEST SCIENCE FICTION STORIES OF H. G. WELLS, H. G. Wells. Full novel *The Invisible Man*, plus 17 short stories: "The Crystal Egg," "Aepyornis Island," "The Strange Orchid," etc. 303pp. 5⅜ × 8½. (Available in U.S. only)
21531-8 Pa. $4.95

AMERICAN SAILING SHIPS: Their Plans and History, Charles G. Davis. Photos, construction details of schooners, frigates, clippers, other sailcraft of 18th to early 20th centuries—plus entertaining discourse on design, rigging, nautical lore, much more. 137 black-and-white illustrations. 240pp. 6⅛ × 9¼.
24658-2 Pa. $5.95

ENTERTAINING MATHEMATICAL PUZZLES, Martin Gardner. Selection of author's favorite conundrums involving arithmetic, money, speed, etc., with lively commentary. Complete solutions. 112pp. 5⅜ × 8½.
25211-6 Pa. $2.95

THE WILL TO BELIEVE, HUMAN IMMORTALITY, William James. Two books bound together. Effect of irrational on logical, and arguments for human immortality. 402pp. 5⅜ × 8½.
20291-7 Pa. $7.50

THE HAUNTED MONASTERY and THE CHINESE MAZE MURDERS, Robert Van Gulik. 2 full novels by Van Gulik continue adventures of Judge Dee and his companions. An evil Taoist monastery, seemingly supernatural events; overgrown topiary maze that hides strange crimes. Set in 7th-century China. 27 illustrations. 328pp. 5⅜ × 8½.
23502-5 Pa. $5.95

CELEBRATED CASES OF JUDGE DEE (DEE GOONG AN), translated by Robert Van Gulik. Authentic 18th-century Chinese detective novel; Dee and associates solve three interlocked cases. Led to Van Gulik's own stories with same characters. Extensive introduction. 9 illustrations. 237pp. 5⅜ × 8½.
23337-5 Pa. $4.95

Prices subject to change without notice.

Available at your book dealer or write for free catalog to Dept. GI, Dover Publications, Inc., 31 East 2nd St., Mineola, N.Y. 11501. Dover publishes more than 175 books each year on science, elementary and advanced mathematics, biology, music, art, literary history, social sciences and other areas.